UNRAVELING
THE
ADD/ADHD
FIASCO

UNRAVELING
THE
ADD/ADHD
FIASCO

Successful Parenting Without Drugs

DR. DAVID B. STEIN

Andrews McMeel
Publishing
Kansas City

04 05 RDH 10 9 8 7 6 5 4 3

Library of Congress Cataloging-in-Publication Data

Stein, David B.
   Unraveling the ADD/ADHD fiasco : successful parenting without drugs / David B. Stein.
      p. cm.
   Includes bibliographical references.
   ISBN 0-7407-1859-2 (pbk.)
      1. Attention-deficit hyperactivity disorder—Alternative treatment.
   2. Parenting. 3. Hyperactive children—Behavior modification. I. Title.

RJ506.H9 S683 2001
618.92'8589—dc21
                                                        2001022654

To my wonderful children,
who have given me so much joy
and meaning in my life:
Kevin, thirteen, Alex, fifteen, and
Heidi, twenty-seven

Contents

CONTENTS

Foreword

by John K. Rosemond, M.S.

F OR ALMOST TWO DECADES I have witnessed a dark—I'll be so bold as to term it evil—trend in psychology and psychiatry. I have watched, often incredulous, as members of these two respected professions mass-marketed two nonexistent diseases, Attention Deficit Disorder (ADD) and Attention Deficit Hyperactivity Disorder (ADHD), to the American public. The success of this propaganda effort has resulted in the victimization of millions of parents and children. Worse has been the elevation of amphetamines— in street slang, "speed"—to legitimate status when used in the so-called treatment of children who have received this diagnosis. Worse still is the fact that many, if not most, of these children's parents are actually convinced that the nature of the "disease" their children supposedly have necessitates the use of these dangerous drugs, often given in dosage levels that would satisfy a street addict.

In the mid '80s, I began noticing that more and more children who were clearly undisciplined were being diagnosed with ADHD. I wrote a newspaper column expressing my alarm and my feeling that the epidemic of children with alarmingly short attention spans (which is not debatable) was the result of parenting practices foisted upon the American public by mental health professionals. It is worse than ironic that bad child-rearing advice from psychologists and other professional know-it-alls has resulted in a generation of children with poor self-control, and that American parents have become persuaded that their children can be saved only by going to the very people who dispensed this bad advice. In 1987, we were told that approximately 3 percent of children had ADD/ADHD. Today, some 10 percent of children—more than *two million*—have been so diagnosed. This is a testament to the power of the most disingenuous secular religion ever conceived: psychology.

How did psychologists and psychiatrists manage to convince physicians, educators, legislators, and parents that these drugs were the only hope for their wretchedly diseased children? Why has the psychological community been reluctant to recommend powerful behavioral treatments of the sort Dr. Dave Stein recommends in this book? Could it be psychologists and other mainstream mental health professionals realize that by admitting the facts, that is,

- ADD/ADHD does not qualify as a disease, and
- powerful behavioral methods (otherwise simply known as "effective discipline") have proven more valuable than drugs in the treatment of the children in question,

their standards of living would suffer greatly? Could it be that these supposedly caring champions of the mentally ill are motivated chiefly by the almighty dollar? Say it isn't so, but I suggest it is. The professionals who have bet the farm on ADD/ADHD will do anything to suppress the truth and continue reaping the rewards of their highly sophisticated con-artistry, a description of which boils down to one word: psychobabble.

Meanwhile, I have waited for someone to step forward and do something meaningful and substantive about this problem—to truly come to the aid of these children and their families. At last, my faith has been rewarded! Dr. Dave Stein—a psychologist no less—has written a book that lays to waste the mythology behind the marketing of ADD/ADHD. But he doesn't stop there. He also offers treatment alternatives that really work. Dr. Dave is a member of the team of professionals who answer questions from parents on my Web site, www.rosemond.com. Time and time again, I've read testimonials from the parents he has helped. That Dr. Dave, as he is known, is able to "cure" ADD/ADHD children over the Internet is irrefutable proof that these disorders are not diseases that require medical treatment and, furthermore, that good old-fashioned discipline of the sort that once blessed the lives of nearly all American children (before we became a "psychological society") is powerful stuff that still works. It helped make America strong, and it can bring America back from the precipice. There's still time.

Parents, if you want real facts and real help, then this is the book for you. I do not endorse this book lightly. I was first drawn to Dr. Stein's previous book, *Ritalin Is Not the Answer: A Drug-free, Practical Program for Children Diagnosed with ADD and ADHD.* What he presented made sense to me, but it took a pediatrician friend of mine who subjected Dr. Dave's program to rigorous clinical testing to convince me that the Caregivers' Skills Program (CSP) really works. This book takes up where *Ritalin Is Not the Answer* left off.

The book makes no claim to be a miracle. Dr. Dave makes it quite clear that if you wish your child to benefit, you will have to roll up your sleeves and put in some hard parenting work. In short, if you want Dave's Caregivers' Skills Program to work, you will have to work, work, work at it! If you do, you will begin to see improvements within two weeks, and if you keep work, work, working, you should see dramatic—I'll say it again: DRAMATIC—improvement in four. All accomplished without drugs. In fact, as Dr. Dave points out, drugs do not advance an impulsive, driven child's rehabilitation. They prevent it.

This book has begun to renew my faith in the profession of psychology. Not in its current state, mind you, but in a hopeful sense. Specifically, I hope that more and more psychologists will be inspired by Dr. Dave's groundbreaking work to join the psycho-heresy revolution. Speaking as one who's been a psycho-heretic for more than twenty years, it's the only way to live. Like myself, Dr. Dave is able to get a good night's sleep.

If you'd like to talk to Dr. Dave personally, you now know where to find him.

John K. Rosemond, M.S., is a psychologist, the author of ten parenting best-sellers, a syndicated columnist, a husband of thirty-three years, a father of two adult children, and a grandfather of four wild and wonderful boys and a sweet little girl.

Foreword

by S. DuBose Ravenal, M.D., F.A.A.P.

As a practicing pediatrician with a heavy interest and involvement in behavioral issues, I have found Dr. Stein's former book, *Ritalin Is Not the Answer*, to be a fascinating and helpful resource. Having run across the title in the process of trying to sort out the numerous confusing issues faced in managing children's ADD/ADHD behaviors, I was initially curious, though skeptical, since his writing challenges much of what has been accepted at face value about managing ADHD. Because the ideas and arguments expressed in his former book are so intuitively logical with regard to the behavioral management of this syndrome, I cautiously began to offer this perspective to select parents who were hesitant to resort to stimulant medications for their child's problem behaviors. When several children with criteria for ADHD by *DSM-IV* responded well, my interest grew. Further reading and communication with Dr. Stein fueled my belief that the CSP approach is valid and that many with ADD/ADHD behaviors can be effectively managed without needing to use stimulant medication.

Unraveling the ADD/ADHD Fiasco is a welcome addition to *Ritalin Is Not the Answer* and brings several significant additions to an approach that many parents readily embrace as controversy and confusion about ADD/ADHD mount in both lay and professional communities. Having had the opportunity now to engage in extended dialogue with Dr. Stein, as well as to apply his approach to an increasing number of families facing ADD/ADHD issues, I am convinced that many of his arguments that challenge conventional ADD/ADHD "wisdom" are true and warrant serious consideration. Having successfully used Dr. Stein's approach, I am now convinced that many widely held but unsubstantiated assumptions are untrue. These false assumptions include that ADD/ADHD is a disease or is caused by a physical or chemical abnormality; that stimulant medication should be the mainstay of an effective long-term way of managing ADHD; and that the currently popular behavioral management techniques based on material reinforcers and providing excessive external structure (prompts, reminders, environmental manipulation, and token economies) contribute to effective management. I now know from Dr. Stein's approach that indeed there is a better way.

Noteworthy and commendable additions to *Ritalin Is Not the Answer* found in *Unraveling the ADD/ADHD Fiasco* include the following:

- The chapter on the definition of disease and implications for the concept of the basic nature of ADD/ADHD is thought-provoking.

- The chapter on the concept and application of Time Out includes several useful differences from how Time Out is often conceived or used.
- Discussions of effective parenting practices, with an emphasis on social reinforcement and nurturing parent-child relationships, are welcome and provide a rich balance.

In conclusion, Dr. Stein is to be commended for a work that promises to throw some light on the ADD/ADHD controversy and offer hope to parents and professionals who struggle to help the increasing number of children who are being identified with problems of inattention and misbehavior fueling a national explosion in ADD/ADHD. In my practice I now use Dr. Stein's books as behavioral prescription alternatives, and I recommend that my fellow practitioners give serious consideration to doing the same.

Acknowledgments

WRITING A BOOK is, by itself, an arduous task, but when you are disagreeing with the Zeitgeist of the professional community it becomes an overwhelming one. I feel very passionately that many unsavory things have occurred in the effort to convince the public and the professional community about things that are blatantly wrong and immoral. Had the good Lord not brought certain individuals across my path, I may have long ago given up this battle.

I am most indebted to Professor Steve Baldwin of the University of Teeside, United Kingdom. He was the first to recognize the merit in my work. He tirelessly worked to establish a drug-free treatment clinic at his university, using my treatment methods. He succeeded in getting this clinic funded by the government just a few months before his untimely death in a train crash in England. I miss his brilliance, his energy, and his integrity. I am left alone to finish much of the work that he and I started, and it is painful.

Dr. Dubose Ravenel came into my life after the publication of my book *Ritalin Is Not the Answer*. A simple phone call was the beginning of a marvelous friendship. He asks questions that make me think of new things, and he constantly brings important research and controversial issues to my attention. In other words, he keeps me on my toes. His energy is infectious and often helps to sustain me through difficult times. Most important, he believes in my work, and having an individual with such deep integrity and conviction on my side has been a blessing.

Courage and clarity of thought barely describe writer and columnist John Rosemond. He has dared to differ with the psychobabble of mainstream psychology and psychiatry. Recognizing the folly of what has been happening in the ADD/ADHD arena, he has bravely and publicly championed and supported my work. I respect his beliefs, his ideas, and his philosophies about child care. He stands for morality and old-fashioned values at a time when the world seems to be going mad. I consider his friendship and advice to be invaluable.

I wish to thank Joyce Trent for the countless hours spent typing, editing, and retyping this manuscript. If it weren't for her, this book would not be a reality.

The friendships and support of Laura Birdsong, Ira Rakoff, and Lois Rakoff have sustained me through many difficult years. Finally, I wish to thank my children, Kevin, Alex, and Heidi, for simply being.

UNRAVELING
THE
ADD/ADHD
FIASCO

CHAPTER 1

Introduction

TREATING WITHOUT DRUGS

D URING THE 1960s and early 1970s, I did my under-
graduate and graduate training in psychology. As part
of my course work, students watched films that documented
the work of pioneer psychologist Ivaar Lovaas. Lovaas was,
at that time, developing behavior modification techniques
for autistic children. Before my eyes I saw miracles unfold.
The incredible gains Lovaas was making with these children astounded me.

Autism is a severe disease of the brain and nervous system. While it is usually present at birth, parents don't
begin to notice that something is terribly wrong with their
child until about the end of the first year. Then the symptoms begin to become apparent. These children can't communicate. They can't speak normally nor can they understand what is being said to them. They are locked in a shell.

Repetitive behaviors, such as spinning a toy, can go on for hours. Hands flapping in midair is a common symptom. The children become wild and out of control if there are even minor changes in their environment. Indeed, they are, tragically, very sick children. Yet Lovaas developed techniques whereby these children's behavior and language skills could be shaped to such an extent that many of them could eventually function normally.

These films and readings in Lovaas's related research excited me and in a large measure helped motivate me toward a career in psychology.

Several years later, when I was teaching and practicing, I got referrals for children who were inattentive and highly misbehaving. At that time, these children fit the diagnosis of hyperkinetic reaction of childhood according to the criteria of the diagnostic manual for psychology and psychiatry, the second edition (the *DSM-II* or *Diagnostic and Statistical Manual, 2d ed.*, published in 1968). I found little information available about how to treat these children behaviorally.

Increasingly, I heard about the use of amphetamine drugs such as Ritalin, Benzedrine, and Dexedrine to control these children's hyperkinetic behaviors. I was both perplexed and vexed. Amphetamines? In children? Surely this couldn't be so. But it was quite real.

To me these children weren't sick. They didn't have anything near the profound degree of pathology present in autistic children. If Lovaas could accomplish behavioral miracles with truly sick autistic children, then surely it would be possible to treat kids who were only overly active and not paying attention. But there weren't any treatments. Nothing was available that worked. Slowly, the idea that ADD/ADHD (Attention Deficit Disorder/Attention

Deficit Hyperactive Disorder) was some kind of illness that could be managed using behavior- and mind-controlling drugs steadily grew popular, and I steadily grew concerned.

Even during my early years of training, psychologists and psychiatrists tried to convince both the professional community and the public that inattentive and overactive children had a disease. This means that something is terribly wrong with their brain or nervous system that causes their inattention and misbehavior. There was not a shred of evidence to support such a claim: I didn't accept that these children had some sort of disease. They weren't at all like autistic children, who were completely out of touch with reality. Inattentive and highly misbehaving children were and are well in touch with reality. They know what they do is wrong. But at that time, psychiatry saw all behavior problems as diseases. If someone was depressed because of the loss of a loved one or a job, that person was considered to have a disease. If a child was anxious about schoolwork, he was considered to have a disease. Typically, the obvious solution for having a disease was medication. Medicines, I thought, were meant to heal, but the amphetamines used on children with attentional problems didn't heal—they controlled.

Then things got "curiouser and curiouser," as in *Alice in Wonderland.*

From the late 1970s to this very day, massive campaigns were undertaken to *prove* that attentional disorders were diseases. Poor research, using any shred of evidence to convince both the public and the professional community that these children had a disease, escalated. This campaign seemed to have a political agenda rather than practicing objective and responsible science.

5

A coincidental second campaign also emerged trying to convince the public and the professional community that Ritalin and other amphetamines were innocuous, mild, safe drugs and that they were "medicines" for treating ADD/ADHD. These drugs were viewed in a casual way, and the message was that no one need be concerned about their effects on the developing bodies of children.

The campaigns have been succeeding. Ritalin and related drugs are selling at an alarming rate: billions of dollars are changing hands. Ten percent of our children, over two million, are now on these drugs, and their use is increasing dramatically.

The popularization of the disease notion had other ramifications. By convincing psychologists, psychiatrists, and educators that attentional disorders were diseases, research on behavioral treatments veered in the wrong direction. Instead of trying to completely remediate the problem behaviors, as Lovaas did with autistic children, treatments took the form of merely supplementing drug therapy. Treatments were not designed to make these children think and function fully. Instead, because the children were viewed as diseased, handicapped, and helpless, behavioral treatments were designed to augment the effects of the drugs, rather than to truly ameliorate the problem.

It was believed that these children were so impaired they needed all the assistance adults could give them in the forms of coaching, reminding, coaxing, prompting, giving individual attention, coddling, and assisting. All of this, actually, only helps to convince the children that they are sick and helpless. These behavioral techniques reinforce and handicap their inability to think or behave without constant outside assistance. As we'll see throughout this book, currently popular behavioral treatments actually make ADD/ADHD children worse. They increasingly become highly dependent on constant help and, worst of all, they become more and more reliant on drugs to function.

How ironic it is that at the very time we are fighting the worst drug epidemic in this country's history, we are feeding our children these very same forms of drugs under the guise of treatment! And these drugs do not "heal," they "control."

Few issues in child health have become as inflammatory, contentious, and controversial as that of ADD/ADHD and the use of Ritalin. Why has it become commonplace to put amphetamines in the bodies of almost 10 percent of our children? As I said at the 1998 American Psychological Association (APA) Conference in San Francisco, "We can do better than this," meaning my fellow psychologists. We can engineer better and more effective behavioral treatments than we have been doing thus far. That's what this book is all about—the introduction of a new behavioral approach that can work as effectively with ADD/ADHD children as Lovaas's technique did with autistic children.

GIVE ME ALTERNATIVES

Numerous physicians have said to me, "Give me alternatives!" That is precisely what this book is all about. Unlike other books on the subject of ADD/ADHD, this book offers a full program of nondrug, behavioral treatment alternatives called the Caregivers' Skills Program (CSP). What is presented here gives a true, workable treatment alternative to Ritalin—a first line of defense for parents, physicians, psychologists, and educators. I ask physicians

7

to hold off writing a prescription for Ritalin and instead write the name of this book. Change the priority of treatment recommendations. An effective behavioral approach is available, and Ritalin can be lowered in the hierarchy of treatment choices. Now parents have a choice available to them. Psychologists can help parents implement this choice. Educators can take encouragement from this program because a pill only controls the children. The Caregivers' Skills Program helps the child learn and develop a whole new and healthier pattern of behaving and thinking that can produce permanent changes, so that never again will the child disrupt the learning environment of other children. With this program, everyone can win—the physicians, the parents, the psychologists, the educators, and most important of all, the children.

The CSP is designed to train parents and other people who take care, that is, caregivers, of ADD/ADHD children in everything necessary to remediate and eliminate the patterns of ADD/ADHD behaviors and thinking.

But this book offers more. We're going to review and make sense out of the mountainous volume of confusing contradictory research, concepts, and theories about ADD/ADHD. We're going to decipher and debunk many of the myths surrounding these disorders.

I hope by the end of this book you will better understand the controversies, have a clearer picture of what is happening in ADD/ADHD research, and be able to parent your children to the point where they are well behaved, great to be around, and much healthier and happier. What Lovaas did without drugs for truly "sick" children, we can do with "nonsick" ADD/ADHD children. This can be done, and together we will do it—without any drugs.

William or "William the Terrible"

William was three years old when he first came to me. My immediate concern was that my techniques work best at from five to eleven years. It didn't take long for my soft side to take over and commiserate with the misery of his parents. William was an unbelievable terror. He literally tore my office to shreds, throwing objects off my desk and scattering important papers. His parents tried desperately to get him under control, but William would have none of it. His mother chased him around the room trying to grab him. She threatened him with spanking. William laughed with glee and continued his spree.

He soon targeted my books, which are dear to me as the tools of my trade. Fortunately, Mom tackled him in time and wrestled him back to her chair, trying to contain him on her lap. William then proceeded to whimper, whine, and struggle, trying to escape Mom's vicelike grip. Dad just sat there looking embarrassed. William began to have a severe tirade. He screamed and kicked and yelled and cried. Ultimately he hit the floor with one of the greatest temper tantrums I ever witnessed.

Believe it or not, I wanted this case. Indeed, William would be a great challenge. He was a terror, and I couldn't have asked for two more highly motivated parents than his.

They had read every book they could get their hands on and admitted that the books only made them more confused. They tried everything, but nothing worked. Out of desperation they went to a child psychiatrist, who told the parents in less than fifteen minutes that William had the disease of ADHD and that Ritalin was the only answer.

Both parents were distressed to put their three-year-old child on an amphetaminelike drug. A neighbor, whose child I had successfully treated, suggested they call me.

For William's parents, I opened a copy of the recent *Physicians' Desk Reference* (PDR), which reviews all prescribed medications, and showed them where it said that Ritalin should not be prescribed for children under the age of six. They were shocked and angry.

I explained the alternative of my teaching them the Caregivers' Skills Program (CSP). Without hesitation, they agreed to undergo the five or six sessions it would take for me to train them. Within two weeks after completing the training in the CSP, they had a normal, well-behaved little boy. True story? Yes! Miracle? No! Diligent work for the parents? Yes!

Not only were William's parents relieved to have him well behaved, but they felt considerably more confident and secure in their parenting skills. They clearly understood what to expect of their child and how to make it happen. At their last session they said, "He seems so much happier."

You are about to embark on the same journey. If Lovaas could control autistic children, we can certainly control ADD/ADHD children. If "William the Terrible" can be controlled, then any child can be controlled. *And no medication is necessary!* By the end of this journey, you too will be able to say, "He seems so much happier." You will be too.

CHAPTER 2

Amphetamines

You're probably reading this book because you are concerned about your child who is taking Ritalin, or a related drug, or because it has been recommended that you start your child on one. As with most parents I've met, you're uncomfortable and confused. "What should I do?" haunts you daily.

I believe it's a myth that most parents want a quick fix with drugs. But only now, with this book and my previous book, *Ritalin Is Not the Answer: A Drug-free, Practical Program for Children Diagnosed with ADD or ADHD*, are parents learning about a real and effective alternative. In order to choose between Ritalin and what I offer, you must be an informed consumer. Therefore, this chapter will review some important information about the family of stimulant drugs and about Ritalin, the one most frequently prescribed. Armed with this information, you can make a more educated choice.

STIMULANT DRUGS

Stimulant drugs are divided into two categories: (1) the minor stimulants and (2) the major stimulants.

The minor stimulants are commonly used as everyday energizers or "pick-me-ups." They are found in many common products. Caffeine is found in coffee, theobromine in chocolate (caffeine is also usually added), and theophylline in tea. While relatively safe, even these drugs can be risky because they increase heart rate, increase blood pressure, and constrict blood vessels. Perhaps your physician told you to cut out drinking coffee. I promised myself that, if my physician ever told me to stop drinking coffee, which I love as a morning beverage, I'd let him have it. He did and I did. It's a good thing we're good friends.

The major stimulants are serious business. They are described in all the textbooks I've ever used for teaching my psychopharmacology course as the most psychologically addicting drugs known. The two types of major stimulants are the amphetamines and cocaine.

Amphetamines are very popular as street drugs and, according to the International Narcotics Control Board (1996), Ritalin has also become popular on the streets. Slang terms for these drugs include "speed," "uppers," "copilots," and "footballs."

In 1970 Congress passed a bill called the Comprehensive Drug Abuse Prevention and Control Act. One purpose of this bill was to restrict and control physicians when they prescribe psychotropic drugs. Drugs were classified into categories called Schedules, ranging from I, which includes drugs that are so addictive that doctors are restricted from any prescription writing, to Schedule V, for drugs with little potential for abuse that can be sold without prescription. Schedule II drugs are highly restricted because they have some medical use but also have very high potential for abuse and addiction. Included in this category are amphetamines (including Ritalin), opium, morphine, and cocaine. Ritalin is not precisely an amphetamine; it's a tad bit different. Pharmacologically, it is closer to cocaine. In hospitals these drugs must be kept in a locked safe to which only the head nurse on the unit has the key. The newer Controlled Substances Analogue Enforcement Act of 1986 still classifies Ritalin in Schedule II.

While Ritalin is one of the mildest of the Schedule II drugs, it still has quite a high addictive potential. There are drugs below this level in Schedules III, IV, and V; therefore, Ritalin is high on the addictive scale. Also included in Schedule II are other drugs used to control ADD/ADHD: Dexedrine (dextroamphetamine), Desoxyn (methamphetamine), and Adderall (amphetamine plus d-amphetamine). Each of these drugs is also classified as Schedule II by the International Narcotics Control Board (1996a). The World Health Organization (WHO) of the United Nations considers the abuse potential of each of these drugs, again including Ritalin, as being equal to cocaine's. In fact, the action of Ritalin in the body is identical to cocaine (LaHaze 1998; DeGrandpre 1999).

IS RITALIN A GATEWAY DRUG?

Parents often ask if Ritalin or any of these drugs can be considered gateway drugs, that is, can lead to use of more powerful, addicting drugs. There are several components to this answer.

My first response is, gateway to what? All Schedule II drugs are already there—near the top of the heap of potentially addictive drugs.

The second part of my answer is that we have no way of knowing which child has a potential risk for becoming addicted to drugs. There is no psychological test for this, and neither is there a medical test. Our treatment success rate for drug addiction is abysmal. If your child is at risk, then any of the Schedule II drugs can trigger an addiction from which there may be no return.

The third part of the answer involves the scientific research on the issue of addiction. There are some studies that seem to show no difference in the addiction rate for children who have taken these drugs versus children who never took them (Biederman, Wilens, and others 1997). Then there are the veiled studies, where one has to do some very careful reading and interpreting. These studies show an early onset of substance abuse in ADHD children when they reach adolescence (Millerger, Biederman, and others 1997) and a high rate of risk for substance abuse for adults who were diagnosed as ADHD as children (Barkley and others 1990; Mannuzza and others 1991). Yet in many of these studies the fact that these ADHD children were on drugs for many years is either not mentioned or dismissed as irrelevant, although being on these drugs may be what truly leads to early drug abuse. Why would experienced researchers make such careless errors of omission? If these studies are accurate, that ADD/ADHD children have a higher rate of substance abuse as adolescents and adults, then that means they are an *at risk* population. Being at risk or having a predisposition to abuse drugs is, therefore, all the more reason to not put these drugs into their systems in the first place.

My fourth point is that to me these research arguments are not as important as mere common sense. Why take the risk of giving Schedule II drugs to children if you don't have to? It's *common sense* that if you teach children to take drugs to manage their behavior and emotions, they are learning drug taking to manage their lives. If we're afraid to have our children drink alcohol or smoke marijuana, then why shouldn't we be afraid for them to consume amphetamines? There are no well-conducted, carefully controlled studies on this addiction issue.

In our society, we have a strange, dualistic way of conceptualizing these drugs. On the one hand we arrest people who consume them without a prescription, and then we freely give them to children. These are the very same drugs about which parents become irate if a child possesses them on the street, and equally as irate if a child refuses to take them when ordered by the doctor. I don't get it.

In my talk at the San Francisco conference, I opened with the following statement:

We're careful about the foods we put in the bodies of our children and then we give them amphetamines.

We're waging a war on tobacco and nicotine being available to our children and then we give them amphetamines.

We're concerned about food additives and preservatives and we give our children amphetamines.

We're waging a war on drugs while at the same time giving our children amphetamines.

I am thoroughly confused.

Why would anyone casually dismiss any of these drugs as not being risky?

Felicia

When I stepped out of my office to greet Mrs. Jones, it was immediately apparent that she was very distressed. She entered my office without smiling and quietly sat down.

When I asked her what might be the matter and what brought her to see me, she put her head in her hands and cried. I offered her tissues, told her it was okay to cry, and waited several minutes until I thought she was ready to talk. She informed me that her nineteen-year-old daughter, Felicia, had been buried the previous weekend after dying from an overdose of cocaine. Mrs. Jones was filled with guilt. Obviously, she was deeply depressed. She was also very angry.

Felicia had been started on Ritalin at age nine because she was not paying attention in class (ADD). Both the school team and the family doctor recommended the drug and told Mrs. Jones it was perfectly safe. The drug didn't work, and the doctor increased the dosage. The drug still didn't produce any change in Felicia's school performance, but at everyone's insistence Mrs. Jones dutifully kept her daughter on the drug. Finally, at age twelve, she tried to take Felicia off the Ritalin, but Felicia did not want to stop. Her behavior became defiant. It soon became apparent that Felicia was consuming other drugs in addition to the Ritalin. She began drinking. She began smoking marijuana.

In high school, Felicia discovered cocaine. At sixteen, she dropped out of school and left home to live in a nearby city. At seventeen, she told her mother she was HIV-positive. At age nineteen, she died of a cocaine-induced heart attack.

Did this nightmare start with Ritalin? I can't say for certain. Would it have happened anyway? I don't know. But Mrs. Jones believed that it started when the system bullied her into starting Felicia on Ritalin. She was angry with the school and with the doctor. I asked if she was considering a lawsuit. She shook her head no. "What good will it do? They'll just make a fool out of me in court," she said.

I saw Mrs. Jones for over two years, at the end of which her deep and painful grieving began to subside. But Mrs. Jones would never fully recover from the loss of her child. What parent could?

I now think to myself, Why do we play Russian roulette with our children when giving them questionable drugs of such intensity?

A BRIEF HISTORY OF AMPHETAMINES

It may be useful to review the background of the development of amphetamines because certain periods in the history of amphetamines help highlight the risks of these drugs. Amphetamine was first synthesized in 1887 by German pharmacologist L. Edeleano. Other related compounds were developed after 1910. In 1927 Gordon Alles, a pharmacology researcher searching for a treatment for asthma, developed Benzedrine. He self-administered the drug and described that it not only helped with his breathing but also reduced his fatigue, increased his alertness, and *made him feel euphoric.* In 1932, the drug company Smith, Kline & French introduced Benzedrine as a nonprescription inhaler for nasal decongestion. In America the drug quickly became popular for recreational use and began to be abused by many. This continued until 1949 when it could no longer be sold over the counter; it had to be prescribed by a physician.

In 1937 Benzedrine began to be prescribed both for treating overactive children and for treating narcolepsy. Ritalin was synthesized in the mid-1940s and was approved for prescription availability by the FDA (Food and Drug Administration) in 1955. Ritalin and related drugs became fairly popular for the treatment of overactive children during the 1960s. Witters and others (1992) describe the '60s as "the doctor feel good" era, when physicians were overly casual about prescribing all types of powerful medications, including amphetamines. The American Medical Association (AMA) claimed that no "serious reactions" could be observed in amphetamines, which was blatantly false. Doctors began prescribing from the family of amphetamine drugs for "obesity, alcoholism, bedwetting, depression, schizophrenia, morphine and codeine addiction, nicotinism, heart block, head injuries, sea sickness, persistent hiccups, and caffeine mania" (Witters and others 1992).

In World War II, amphetamines were issued to soldiers in Germany, Japan, England, and Sweden (neutral). After the war, each of these countries experienced marked abuse epidemics of amphetamines. It took ten years of passing restrictive laws for the problem to be brought under control in these countries. However, the United States, even though it knew of the problem, issued amphetamines to troops during the Korean War. And sure enough, after the war we had a similar abuse epidemic that lasted until the Controlled Substances Act was passed in 1970, when restrictions were placed on physicians' prescription writing.

I hope this brief history alerts you that when these drugs become easily available, large-scale abuse ensues. Are we repeating history? Now that these drugs proliferate in our schools, we are hearing reports from the media and the Drug Enforcement Agency (DEA) that Ritalin is the most recreationally abused drug on high school and college campuses. Kids grind the pill into a fine powder and then snort it just like cocaine. They get a high that is almost identical to cocaine. Soon they will learn they can get the same effect with any of the other Schedule II drugs. Can this happen to your child?

AMPHETAMINE RISKS

Are there other serious risks to children, aside from abuse and addiction, from taking amphetamines? Yes! We don't even know all the risks involved with Ritalin and related drugs because there are almost no long-term studies available. We don't know what will happen ten, twenty, or more years later after several years of taking these drugs as a child. Cylert was considered the mildest and safest of these drugs and is the only one being prescribed that is classified as a Schedule IV drug. But the manufacturer, Abbott Laboratories, was required by the FDA to issue a warning letter to all physicians that deaths had occurred as a result of liver failure. Sales of Cylert are dropping dramatically. The mildest of all these drugs is only recently being discovered to contribute to death.

All the amphetamines, including Ritalin, cause the children's bodies to markedly slow down their normal growing process. This is called *growth suppression*. These drugs directly lower the production of growth hormones (Yudofsky 1991), which then causes all parts of a child's body to grow at a less than normal rate. This growth suppression includes weight and height (Mates and Gittelman 1983), as well as brain and head size (Nasrallah 1986; Pizzi and others 1986; Breggin 1998). Shaywitz and others (1983) state, "The adverse effect on growth hormone is so regular and predictable that it can be used as a measure of whether or not the Ritalin is active in the child's body" (p. 26, cited in Breggin 1998). "Even a child's sexual maturation is impaired" (Jacobovitz 1990).

Please reflect on this issue. Your child's body is extremely delicately balanced. Most parents take great pains to make sure their children's bodies are well taken care of. We check for fat content in foods, we read labels for food preservatives, we support the campaign to prevent our children from taking nicotine and tobacco products, and yet we permit them to consume worse drugs, which interfere with the entire normal growing process. It is possible that, when long-term studies are finally conducted, there will be a very serious price to pay for prescribing these drugs for children.

After the drugs are stopped, growth resumes. We don't

know if the resumption ever catches up to its proper potential level. Weiner (1982) indicates that we have no way of knowing how big or how tall a child would have become if he had never taken the drug. What effect does this "stop and go" process have on a child's body and brain? We don't know that either!

As you may be aware, your child's brain is not fully developed at birth. The human brain continues a normal course of development until the age of twelve, when it finally reaches full maturation. Vital events occur during these twelve years. Neural pathways develop that are affected by what they learn and by their environment. Critically and carefully balanced levels of the chemicals in the nervous system and brain develop. Nerve cells develop precise configurations called *receptor sites*, which are crucial to the healthy functioning of the nervous system. The brain grows in size, and critical changes occur in its anatomy on a fairly precise normal development schedule. Growth suppression followed by a spurt of catching up interferes with this normal and gradual process. Should we be messing with this in our children?

Doctors have come up with a way of trying to reduce this growth inhibition problem, which is called *drug holidays*, where the child is given the drug only on days he is in school. These children usually don't take the drugs at night, on weekends, holidays, or during summer vacations. These holidays are recommended only for children whose behavior isn't severely disruptive during the "holidays." Drug holidays only reduce the risks, however; they don't eliminate them. If these drugs were as safe as doctors lead us to believe, then why do they believe in having drug holidays in the first place?

Ritalin and related drugs also impair the crucial development of the sexual system (Jacobovitz and others 1990). Think about this. Think of all the crucial changes in the development of sexual organs, breasts, menstrual cycle, testicles, sexual hormones, and change of voice that must unfold on a set time schedule for sexual maturation to proceed normally. We honestly do not know very much about the long-term implications of inhibiting normal sexual growth patterns during crucial developmental stages.

A very recent, unique long-term study (Auci 1997) indicates that the immune system may also be impaired by long-term use of these drugs. Think about that—the immune system, which protects your child from diseases. Doctors are reporting that children on these drugs seem to be presenting more frequently problems with colds, bronchitis, and even pneumonia. More long-term studies are desperately needed to find out what happens to the developing bodies of children who are kept on these drugs.

Long-term detrimental side effects may appear after years of remaining on the drugs, or even years later after stopping the drugs. Little is known about their long-term effects. But we know a great deal about short-term effects, detrimental problems that emerge within weeks or even immediately after beginning the drugs.

Table 2.1 lists some of the short-term side effects of amphetamines and Ritalin. The percentage of cases affected is also listed.

There are two short-term side effects worth highlighting. First is cognitive toxicity, which involves the drugs' capacity to improve the ability to learn simple, rote memory types of tasks, like addition and subtraction, while it impairs the ability to perform complex and abstract think-

TABLE 2.1

Percentage of Cases Showing Short-Term Side Effects

Symptom	Ritalin	Amphetamines
Depression	8. 7%	39. 0%
Confusion	3. 9	0. 3
Mood changes	10. 0	less than 1. 0
Irritability	17. 3	25. 0
Agitation & restlessness	6. 7	10. 0
Tics (dykinesias)	9. 0	less than 1. 0
Lethargy & drowsiness	18. 8	11. 5
Loss of appetite	26. 9	23. 1
Loss of weight	13. 5	29. 5
Nausea	11. 6	5. 5
Blood pressure increases	15. 8	10. 0
Cardiac arrhythmia	5. 5	less than 1. 0
Angina	4. 4	less than 1. 0
Abdominal pains	11. 6	5. 5
Cognitive toxicity	40. 0	40. 0

Sources: Breggin 1998; Maxmen & Ward 1991; Physicians' Desk Reference 2000

ing tasks, such as solving science problems or writing essays and poetry. This occurs in over 40 percent of all children taking these drugs (Breggin 1998; Swanson and others 1993). Now think about that. These drugs are taken to improve school performance. They do control conduct, and they do improve performance on simple and repetitive tasks. But they interfere with higher, more complex learning tasks in a large percentage of children. I call this "win the battle and lose the war." Our highest thinking abilities are thus impaired while on these drugs.

Another problem that occurs rarely when lower doses

are prescribed, in less than 1 percent of patients, but more frequently at higher doses, is called toxic psychosis. In these cases the poisonous effects of the drugs cause the child to lose touch with reality and become psychotic. I've witnessed this actually happening on several occasions during my career, and it's terrifying.

At this point you may be dismayed if your child is taking one of these drugs. Indeed, you should be. Drugs of this intensity should be used as a treatment of last resort. Unfortunately, because of the ineffectiveness of most currently available behavioral treatments, they are being used as a treatment of first choice.

I can think of only two reasons for using amphetamines in children: when well-designed behavioral treatments fail, or when parents don't want to take the time or effort to learn how to work with their child. Since you're reading this book, my hunch is you're not part of this latter group.

We'll see in chapter 5 that currently popular behavioral programs are not well designed. All too often I have heard, as I bet you have, the frequent claim that "the best approach is the combination of behavioral techniques with medication." Nonsense! Currently popular behavioral approaches are poorly designed, and they do not work unless the amphetamines are added. In fact, current behavioral techniques can be completely discarded, because the same results can be gotten with the drugs alone. When current behavior programs are used alone, they not only don't work, they actually make the children worse. I'm offering you a completely different, viable, and real drug-free alternative.

The Caregivers' Skills Program (CSP) is carefully designed and carefully researched, and it works. This is the only comprehensive and effective program of its kind. In chapter 5, I'll explain to you the differences in the CSP approach and other currently available behavioral and parenting approaches.

In the next chapter, we'll explore the very complex issues of whether ADD/ADHD is a disease, a biological disorder, or simply a pattern in children who are normal but tend to be more active and less motivated to pay attention.

CHAPTER 3

Are ADD and ADHD Diseases?

A GROWING NUMBER of lawsuits are being filed against pharmaceutical companies, claiming conspiracies to market and sell addicting drugs to children diagnosed as ADD/ADHD. These suits are being initiated by some of the law firms that fought the tobacco companies. The conspiracy issues focus on the alleged use of underhanded tactics by the drug companies, of systematic misinformation and disinformation to orchestrate a huge multibillion-dollar market by targeting children for the sale of amphetamines.

At the center of these alleged conspiracies has been the effort to misuse science to convince the public that ADD/ADHD are diseases, that the logical cure is drugs, and that these drugs are perfectly safe. I hope the last chapter helped you to question the safety of amphetamines.

In this chapter we will attempt to unravel the mystery and confusion surrounding the issue of whether or not attentional disorders are diseases. Don't be dismayed if you've been trying to make sense out of this issue. Many professionals are also confused. Indeed, it is a difficult topic to deal with. The disease issue affects not only ADD/ADHD, but also how we look at and interpret many other psychiatric disorders.

This chapter may be a little bit difficult to work through because the disease versus nondisease issue is complex. The material is presented fully and without simplification in order to assist those parents who wish to understand this controversy completely.

THE PSYCHIATRIC PLAYGROUND

We owe a lot to the pharmaceutical companies. Their funding of research has helped conquer many diseases. But their role in the history of psychiatry has been somewhat suspect.

In mainstream medicine diseases are usually clear. They are clearly detected and measured with scientific instruments. When a drug is used, its effectiveness in eliminating a disease is usually apparent. In psychiatry/psychology, however, where definitions are unclear, concepts are muddled, and what is or is not a disease is controversial, things are different. Being in psychiatry/psychology is often like being Alice in Wonderland.

I once attended a medical insurance company conference where a company executive was reviewing the issue of paying for psychiatric and psychological therapy sessions. He pointed out that when they paid claims for dentists, the disease or abnormality they were treating was clear, the procedures that were used were clear, and when a disease was cured it was also clear. He pointed out that the same could be said for physician insurance claims. But when they reviewed psychiatric/psychological claims, they often didn't know what the hell anyone was talking about.

Because of the lack of clarity and precision, psychiatry and psychology are fertile ground for making any dubious statements designed to market drugs. Psychiatric drugs constrain behavior. Whether they cure or correct any diseases is completely unknown, because we don't even know what a disease is in psychiatry and psychology. Nevertheless, are these drugs beneficial? Under some circumstances the answer is yes. They can be helpful with painful feelings, such as anxiety or depression. They can calm down schizophrenic patients and help them function. They can help control the moods of bipolar (manic-depressive) patients. But they cure nothing; they only control. Most important, these drugs are very powerful and can potentially be very dangerous. They should be used with great restraint and for the shortest time possible. They should not be used when it is completely unnecessary. Unfortunately, pharmaceutical companies have been pursuing some rather questionable practices. They seem to be funding research aimed at labeling more and more behavior problems as diseases, in order to create larger and more lucrative markets for their products. In other words, they are literally manufacturing psychiatric diseases. There seems to be a handful of Nixonian researchers, that is, with borderline integrity, to do their bidding by using science to support all types of bogus and nebulous claims.

Lack of clarity and excessive confusion make psychiatry and psychology a breeding ground for such unsavory research activities. So clever are these researchers with the manipulation of science that even honorable clinicians and researchers have been fooled into accepting distortions as facts. British psychologist H. J. Eysenck once said that psychologists (and psychiatrists) can say anything, because their patients don't die from it. Labeling more and more behavioral problems as diseases justifies the sale of more and more drugs.

While the issues of disease and the unnecessary sale of drugs have been of concern to many, it has become particularly inflammatory ever since the drug companies have begun targeting children for the consumption of amphetamines. It is in this arena that many oppose what the drug companies are doing.

The pharmaceutical companies are sponsoring a massive volume of truly bad research to prove that ADD/ADHD are diseases and that amphetamines are safe. Psychiatry and psychology have refused to police themselves, and therefore it appears that a bunch of lawyers will have to do the job.

ARE ADD/ADHD CHILDREN PHYSICALLY DIFFERENT?

Are children who consistently fail to pay attention (ADD) physically different from other children? Are children who are consistently hyper and frequently misbehaving (ADHD) physically different?

My answer to the question may surprise you, because it's *YES!* But: *Any and all consistent patterns of human behav-*

iors will have different physiological (physical or bodily) patterns from other behavioral patterns. This difference does NOT mean a disease or a biological disorder. It means only that different patterns of all normal behaviors will have different underlying physical patterns.

THE NEW MACHINES

Since the publication of the *DSM-III* in 1980 (the *DSM-IV*, now in use, was published in 1994), a new revolution has happened not only in psychology and psychiatry but also in the fields of medicine and the biological sciences. With the advent of computers, new modern miracle medical machines have appeared, such as CAT scans, MRIs, PET scans, and SPECT scans (see Table 3.1).

With these new machines, we are now detecting subtle changes at the cellular and chemical levels of the body. It is the improper use of these machines that is justifying nonexistent diseases. Researchers are claiming subtle readings as chemical or anatomical causes of behavior that no one else seems to be able to replicate. Even if readings were accurate, which they are not, we often don't know what they mean or what may be causing the physical anomalies to be present. Do these physical changes appear spontaneously? Are they the product of genetics? Are these anomalies causing abnormal behaviors or are they the result of prolonged environmental stress? Are they caused by different patterns of thinking, called cognitions? Are they caused by nutrition or diet? Or are they resulting from the years children participating in the research had been taking the drugs?

Table 3.1

Computerized Medical Machines

CT or CAT Scans—*computerized axial tomography*
Computer-enhanced x-ray machine to detect structural or anatomical abnormalities
MRI—*magnetic resonance imaging*
Similar to CT scans, but more accurate
PET Scans—*positron emission tomography*
Detects energy emitted by cells while metabolizing radioactive glucose
EEG—*electroencephalography*
Detects electrical activity of the brain
Evoked Responses
Computerized averages of EEG responses to stimuli
Echoencephalography
Ultrasound imaging of the brain of children less than two years of age. This is similar to CT and MRI procedures but is less risky and less accurate
SPECT Scans—*single photon emission computed tomography*
Used to detect general information about the blood flow and metabolic functioning of the brain
Electron microscope—*a microscope that can see at the molecular level. Often used in DNA research.*

Source: Berkow, ed., *The Merck Manual* 1997

ABSENCE OF A DEFINITION OF DISEASE

One major problem is interpreting whether the subtle differences in patterns detected by the machines are diseases. There is a gigantic diversity in the patterns of human behavior, and each and every pattern will have a wide range of measurements that show up when reading today's advanced medical machines. Within each range, where does the separation between normal and abnormal begin? For example, do the physiological differences between introverts and extroverts mean that one has a disease and the other doesn't? Do the physiological differences between dependent people and independent people mean one is diseased and the other isn't? Are more active people diseased and less active people not? A recent newspaper article stated that researchers performing MRI studies found that the anatomy of the brains of teenagers was different from that of adults. We can now conclude what we've always suspected—adolescence is a disease!

Linda Seligman (1994) says that the pendulum in psychiatric diagnosis is now swinging back toward the disease days before 1980 and earlier, when everything in the *DSM-I* and *II* was considered a disease. In 1980 the *DSM-III* drastically moved away from the disease model, but with the development of this new technology, since 1980, the pendulum began swinging back to interpreting findings as diseases. Psychology and psychiatry have been taken by surprise. Arguments are growing over whether we view certain newly observed physiological patterns as diseases, and the dispute over the confused interpretations is escalating. If this trend toward disease interpretation continues, then every pattern of human behavior will soon be a disease, and that is absurd! The growing problem is how do we interpret these findings? All of this probably makes the drug companies quite happy, because the more diseases everyone sees, the more drugs they sell.

A major source of the confusion is that in psychology and psychiatry there is no definition of the term *disease*. Let me show you how the members of the committees that developed the *DSM-IV* in 1994 handled the definition dilemma:

> Moreover, although this manual provides a classi-
> fication of mental disorders, it must be admitted
> that no definition adequately specifies precise
> boundaries for the concept of "mental disorders"
> [mental disease]. The concept of mental disorder
> [disease], like many other concepts in medicine
> and science, lacks a consistent operational defini-
> tion that covers all situations. (p. xxi)

And

> In most situations, the clinical diagnosis of a *DSM-
> IV* mental disorder is not sufficient to establish the
> existence for legal purposes of a "mental disorder,"
> "mental disability," "mental disease," or "mental
> defect." (p. xxiii)

With this in mind, perhaps you can see why one psychologist sees a physiological-chemical pattern as a disease
and another sees it as a disorder (or nondisease). This has
remained a moot issue for over one hundred twenty-five
years, awaiting a solution. After having spent several years
on this problem, British professor Steve Baldwin and I
have developed a definition that has been published in an
international medical journal (Stein and Baldwin 2000).
Hopefully, this definition will serve as an anchor to reduce
the continuation of loose speculations over what is or is not
a psychiatric disease.

Children with schizophrenia and autism are so severely

impaired that they cannot control their behaviors *and* they are not in touch with reality. The behavioral patterns of ADD/ADHD do not come anywhere near such drastic patterns. ADD/ADHD children are not out of touch with reality, as are schizophrenic and autistic children.

In addition, the ADD/ADHD physiological-chemical patterns are so subtle that they too must be considered well within normal limits. It doesn't matter for you in using this book, however, because either way what I present here works.

DISEASE THEORIES

As I've stated, historically there have been no satisfactory definitions of disease in psychiatry and psychology. However, I must explain a scientific term to you—*etiology* (British spelling *aetiology*). Etiology means the *cause* of a disease or disorder or behavior pattern. The argument over disease versus no disease is in part an argument over etiology. If researchers can find a physical difference, or etiology, that underlies ADD/ADHD, then they have justified their idea that it's a disease, that is, causative. As we'll soon see, there has been a major scramble to find this etiology, and the search has resulted in a rather extensive list of theories (see Table 3.2).

However, if you've ever looked at lab reports from your doctor's office, you'll notice that there are boundaries or limits of lab findings that separate normal from pathological (or diseased) findings. As I stated, for the physiologies or etiologies (causations) of psychiatric disorders, these boundaries or lines of demarcation have not been established. They don't exist.

TABLE 3.2

Representative Studies of Brain and Nervous System Dysfunction

Area of Brain	Date of Study	Studies Attributing Problem to ADD/ADHD	Date of Study	Studies Attributing Problem to Drugs
*1. brainstem dysfunction	1995	Lahat, E., et al.	1990	Pearson, J., et al.
*2. caudate nucleus dysfunction	1994	Castellanos, F. X., et al.	1985	Unis, A. S., et al.
*3. corpus callosum	1994	Giedd, J. M., et al.	1986	Nasrallah, H., et al.
*4. dopamine	1991	Levy, F.	1995	Jaffe, J.
5. folic acid imbalance	1994	Greenblatt, J. M., et al.		
*6. frontal lobe	1991	Heilman, K. M., et al.	1992	During, M. J., et al.
*7. brain metabolism dysfunction	1993	Zametkin, A. J., et al.	1987	Porrino, L. J., et al.
*8. prefrontal cortex	1993	Amen, K. G., et al.	1985	Unis, A. S., et al.
9. serum lipid	1994	Arnold, L. E., et al.		
*10. serotonin	1998	Murphy, D. A., et al.	1992	Kosten, T. R.

*dysfunction can be caused by drugs

So not only do we not have a proper definition, we don't even have boundaries for causes that clearly state if findings are within or outside normal limits. The wide diversity of normal human behavior patterns means there must be an equally wide set of limits or tolerances for the diversity of etiologies.

Now let's take a look at the search for etiologies, or abnormal physical problems, that supposedly cause ADD/ADHD.

A HISTORY OF THE SEARCH FOR THE DISEASE OF ADD/ADHD

The disease, or biological, theories of ADD/ADHD began in 1902 as a *guess* by an English pediatrician, George Still. He was the first to describe children who were inattentive and highly misbehaving. He didn't see this as a learned pattern of behavior; instead, he saw it as being caused by something wrong with the brain or body. As a physician he was trained to see everything as medically caused, and his interpretation of these children's behaviors was consistent with his medical orientation. Unfortunately, even though no supportive evidence existed, the disease theory for ADD/ADHD had its beginnings.

Around 1923 an outbreak of an encephalitic epidemic left numerous children with this inattentive and hyperactive behavior pattern. Dr. F. G. Ebaugh concluded that perhaps a virus or the encephalitic virus itself caused inflammation or damage to the brain of the children that resulted in this behavior pattern. Again, there was no proof. It was only a guess, but it fueled support for the disease notion.

In 1937, Dr. Charles Bradley noticed that stimulant drugs seemed to subdue the behavior of these highly active and inattentive children. Later this became known as the "paradoxical effect," because he believed that only in these hyper children do we observe this subduing effect. This theory remained popular until fairly recently, when researchers began to discover that stimulant drugs produce this same effect on everybody and anybody. Baldessarini (1988), who is considered one of the world's leading authorities on psychiatric drugs, calls this reasoning *allopathic logic*, meaning that because a drug produces an effect, then there must be a disease. He sees this type of reasoning as false, misleading, and invalid. Anyway, this idea has pretty much faded away; few currently accept the paradoxical effect theory.

In the 1940s, Strauss and Lehtinen (1947) proposed the idea that the cause of these behaviors was some type of minimal brain damage or MBD. But damage was so minimal that no one could find it. This notion has died slowly. One remaining advocate of the MBD notion is Paul Wender, who is a strong advocate of stimulant drugs.

The *DSM-II* was published in 1968 by the American Psychiatric Association, and it used the terms "hyperkinetic reaction of childhood." Words often have two meanings. Denotative meanings are the precise definitions of a word, such as "I see red" meaning I see the color red. Connotative meanings are implied meanings, or emotional reactions to a word, such as "I see red" meaning I'm angry. To most, the term *hyperkinesis* sounds like or connotes a meaning of a disease. Some liked the connotation evoked by the term, but others, mostly psychologists, were not in favor of such pejorative, that is, negative or implied disease, terminology.

As Seligman (1994) stated, in the development of the 1980 version of the *DSM-III* there was a strong current of feeling to move away both from pejorative connotations and from disease concepts that had no support. Researcher Virginia Douglas viewed the behavior problems as resulting from a deficit in attention. The term *attention deficit disorder* (ADD) was settled on. However, while no research that I know of suggests that these terms are pejorative to the public or the professional community, I still feel the term connotes an underlying disease. In fact, I've done a survey to see if the ADD/ADHD term connotes a disease to people, and preliminary results indicate that most people do make such an inference. People make the statement "I have ADD/ADHD," which very much sounds as if they believe they have a disease.

Students constantly come to me requesting special conditions for taking exams or special considerations for taking notes during lecture, such as using tape recorders, because they *have* ADD or ADHD.

A New Label

Since words have connotative meanings, they influence the way we perceive and interpret events and concepts. Perhaps changing the terms ADD and ADHD will help to perceive these behavioral patterns in a very different way. For the term ADD—attention deficit disorder—substitute IA (inattentive), and for ADHD—attention deficit hyperactive disorder—substitute the term HM (highly misbehaving), and notice the change in your perceptions. To me the terms IA/HM, or Inattentive and Highly Misbehaving, help move our interpretations away from the pejorative disease label to a more realistic thought and behavioral disorder. Therefore, for the remainder of this book the terms IA/HM will appear alongside the traditional ADD/ADHD label. Hopefully, the terminology will have an impact on both the public and professional communities and will begin to change our perceptions of these behaviors as diseases.

BARKLEY'S DISEASE CAMPAIGN

After 1980, as medical technology advanced, as I stated earlier many researchers began to use the new machines in the search for the disease or the physiological etiology of ADD/ADHD (IA/HM). The modern champion of the disease quest and the strongest advocate for the use of drugs to treat these children was Russell Barkley (1978). Barkley's 1981 book, *Hyperactive Children: A Handbook for Diagnosis and Treatment*, received widespread attention from both the public and the professional community. Throughout the '80s, Barkley repeated disease-disease-disease-Ritalin-Ritalin-Ritalin, even though not a shred of solid evidence existed to support his disease theory. Later, in 1991, he published a paper claiming that the research of physician Alan Zametkin on PET scan patterns of adults who may have been ADHD as children proved by some convoluted logic that ADHD children's brains are different from those of normal children. Thus, Barkley found much-needed support for his disease campaign.

There have been many complaints about the replicability of Zametkin's findings and about his research methods (Breggin 1998), but to me the most alarming criticism of Zametkin's work is the plain fact that PET scans are not accurate measuring devices. They have not reached a reliable state of technology (Mayberg 1998; Sedvall 1997). For both Barkley and Zametkin to declare a disease from such weak evidence, which then resulted in more and more children being put on drugs, was irresponsible, was scientifically unsound, and was morally wrong.

Nevertheless, the campaign caught on. Soon an avalanche of research to find more support for the disease theory ensued. Table 3.2 indicates that the represented group of studies lists a whole variety, almost a dozen, of diseases implicating various areas of the brain, the nervous system, or the chemistry of the nervous system. If all these studies are accurate, then these children are extraordinarily sick!

There is a major flaw in all these studies. They either indicate that almost all the children in the studies were on stimulant medication at the time of the measurements, or that they had been on the medication for many years prior to the measurements, or many of the studies fail to make any mention of the children's medication histories. I've placed asterisks in Table 3.2 where the medications can either directly or indirectly affect these very same areas of the brain, nervous system, or chemistry. By indirectly, I mean that stimulant drugs suppress physical growth throughout the entire body and decrease the production of growth hormone (Brown and Williams 1976; Joyce and others 1986; Dulcan 1994), resulting in a marked suppression of the growth of the brain and head (Pizzi and others 1986) and weight and height (Mates and Gittelman 1983). This cessation of growth can eventually result in some of the anatomical changes found in some of these studies.

This onslaught of research, the finding of so many dis-

eases, the contamination of the studies, the premature declarations of disease discovery, and the poor quality of many
of these studies reduce the credibility of almost all of them.
Can they all be true and accurate? Or are none of them true
or accurate?

In November 1998 I attended the National Institutes
of Health Consensus Conference on Attention Deficit
Hyperactive Disorders in Bethesda, Maryland. NIH holds
consensus conferences in areas of medicine where diagnoses, research, and treatments yield confusing and inconsistent interpretations. A team of eminent researchers,
writers, and practitioners reviews all aspects of a controversy from presentations by the scientists who have been
producing the research. The task of the team is to clarify
the issues as much as possible. This year the team concluded that the validity of the disease theories, or biological
causes, of ADD/ADHD (IA/HM) was not substantiated by
the evidence. The following is taken from the report:

At this time, we do not have a diagnostic test for
ADHD (biochemical, physiological, anatomical,
genetic, etc.). Therefore, the validity of the disorder continues to be a problem. (p. 3)

Thus, even the National Institutes of Health questions
the reliability and validity of these studies. Please take note
of the following statement made by Russell Barkley (1995)
in one of his more recent books:

Misled by research reports that lab measures have
found differences between ADHD and non-ADHD
children and by the fact that ADHD is a biologi-

cally based disorder, many parents ask for medical tests to confirm the diagnosis of ADHD. At present, there are no lab tests or measures that are of value in making a diagnosis of ADHD, so blood work, urinalysis, chromosome studies, EEGs, averaged evoked responses, MRIs, and computed tomography (CT scans) should not be used routinely in the evaluation of ADHD children. (p. 122)

These machines, according to Barkley, are good enough to make a national declaration of the existence of a disease and to put two million children on amphetamines, but they are not good enough to confirm the disease when a child makes an office visit! Does this scare you? Significantly, Barkley does not mention PET scans, on which he has relied the most. PET scans are even less reliable than any of the other machines he mentions.

At the NIH conference, James Swanson made a statement similar to Barkley's. However, instead of using the term *disease*, he called it a *biological disorder*. There is currently a new trend to abandon the word disease because of a growing lack of credibility for the term, and instead substitute the term biological disorder. Swanson declared a biological disorder in his research but stated that these findings could not be confirmed in office visits or clinical testing. I publicly confronted him at the conference and asked if this was psychobabble or doublespeak. How could he or Barkley make declarations of a biological disorder from their research but not be able to confirm this in routine office visits using the same machines? This is not responsible science.

The *DSM-IV* also supports my interpretation of Barkley's and Swanson's statements: "There are no laboratory tests that have been established as diagnostic in the clinical assessment of Attention Deficit/Hyperactivity Disorder" (p. 81).

Psychiatrist Josephine Wright (1997) states, "But ADHD is not a clearly defined disease, like pneumonia" (p. 2). Yet, she still persists in calling it a disease. Loose use of the term disease results, to me, in children being placed on drugs, and therefore should be avoided while there is the absence of a clear definition of the term disease, or until Baldwin's and my criteria are met.

There are two trends currently taking place in psychology and psychiatry as a result of this questionable pattern of research: first, a number of psychologists and psychiatrists are abandoning the hard-line use of the term disease, and second, they are supporting a softer line, believing there is some degree of physiological difference that, at present, can't be verified. In 1999, DeGrandpre stated that attention deficit disorders are not a "disease or illness," but rather they are a condition that reflects the biochemistry and physiology of the individual's nervous system. This means that they only reflect the biochemical differences of normal people, just as I mentioned earlier. DeGrandpre (1999) stated that because of all the inconsistent results of these studies, we cannot by any stretch of the imagination assume that ADD and ADHD are diseases, and we cannot rely on research and diagnoses that do not clearly define their variables or terms.

At the 1998 American Psychological Association Convention in San Francisco, I debated A. D. Anastopoulos and G. J. DuPaul, both disease advocates and Ritalin proponents. They indicated that ADD/ADHD (IA/HM) may not be a disease, but there are physiological differences and, they added, "Someday we're sure we'll find them." Once again, are they deluding the public and professional community by inferring these are abnormal or disease differences instead of being only differences within the wide range of normal patterns of behavior, as I believe?

With a growing number of skeptics, with a lack of credible research, and with the new NIH statement, the disease issue is wearing down. I hope that what I present here educates the public and my fellow professionals as to what has been going on. Breggin (1998) points out that this disease question has to be dealt with, because the consequences are that more and more children take amphetamines daily in the name of treating the "disease" of Attention Deficit Disorder and Attention Deficit Hyperactive Disorder.

Please bear in mind that any physiological findings I've alluded to are, in reality, very tenuous and questionable at this time. The research is so convoluted and confusing that no one can truly make any sense of it.

THE STRATEGY OF VOLUME

Schlessinger (1998) and DeGrandpre (1999) have called all this research "junk science"; I call it "unethical science." Most of this research is funded by the pharmaceutical companies. Woe to the researcher who doesn't find a disease— he'll have considerable difficulty obtaining grant money for more research. And in medical schools and universities, pressure is on to bring in more and more grant money. The researcher who doesn't can expect few promotions and minimal pay raises (Valenstein 1998). Psychiatric and, recently, psychological scientific journals are increasingly relying on pharmaceutical advertising to remain profitable (Valenstein 1998). Is this not a conflict of ethical interest?

The easy availability of pharmaceutical company research grants underlies the current avalanche of research and spurious findings. Instead of quality, we are being convinced of diseases by overwhelming volume. And it seems to be working. I sadly must say that I can no longer trust what I read in psychiatric and psychological journals. Perhaps these new lawsuits will lead to reform.

The Question of What May Cause Physical Differences

If any findings are ever truly made, it will be difficult to determine if these physiological differences cause the ADHD or if other things caused these underlying physical differences. We know that the environment definitely affects our behavior and our thinking, and it can affect the structure of our nervous system. Stressful lifestyles can produce behavioral, cognitive, *and* physical changes. So can parenting styles. Thinking or cognitive patterns that are the hallmark of ADHD children can produce the physiological differences. I pointed out in one of my research articles (Stein and Baldwin 2000) that the self-induced state of agitation the ADHD child stays in can also produce these physical and biological changes. These all mean that physical changes may be *resultant*, as we discussed earlier. I believe that Josephine Wright (1997) is incorrect when she writes:

During the latter part of the 1960s doctors and researchers began to realize with greater certainty that the symptoms that make up ADHD are biological and possibly genetic in origin—not the result of poor parenting, environment, or children just being "bad." (p. 17)

As you can see from our discussion, this statement is not well founded. It is wishful thinking for those who support the use of Ritalin. Her next sentence states:

The use of stimulants, particularly Ritalin, became increasingly common as parents looked desperately for effective treatment. (p. 17)

My answer to this is that medication is no longer the only available treatment—the Caregivers' Skills Program is equally or even more effective and is a far more healthy alternative for the children.

Remember my position: There are physiological differences in ADD/ADHD (IA/HM) persons, as there are for all forms of human behavior. This does not justify declaration of a disease or a biological disorder, and it does not justify putting amphetamines into children. Ask yourselves: Why are so many psychologists and psychiatrists trying to prove a disease or biological disorder? Why are they fervently trying to justify giving these drugs to children? What is their motive????

GENE AND CHROMOSOME THEORIES

Recently, there has been an increase in the search to discover the genetic or DNA and chromosome components
that may underlie ADD/ADHD (IA/HM). Table 3.3
shows that a pattern similar to that with the disease theories may be emerging. Notice the wide variety of genes
identified as "causing" attentional disorders. The race
appears to be on again.

It's important to note the meaning of this research.
Finding the key genes means finding the ultimate cause of
the physiological abnormalities or diseases the researchers
couldn't justify in the first place. This would mean that

TABLE 3.3

Gene and Chromosome Theories

Gene	Author	Date of Article
Fragile X	National Fragile X Foundation	1998
Dopamine Transporter	Comings, D. E.	1996
Dopamine D4 Receptor		
Dopamine B—hydroxylase		
Dopamine D2 Receptor		
Serotonin 1A Receptor		
Tryptophane 2,3—dioxygenase		
Monoamine Oxygenase A&B		
C 4B	Odell, J. D.	1997
DAT 1	Cook, E. H., et al.	1995
Monosomy AX	Samango-Sprouse, C.	1999

---

biology, not environment, would be the ultimate etiology or causative agent.

DNA findings seem so scientifically impressive and mystifying to both the public and the professional community that a quest is on to make this the new avenue to support disease theories. Right now the genes that affect the production of a neurotransmitter called dopamine, that is, chemicals in the nervous system that increase transmission of electrical impulses within the brain and nervous system, are being favored. Imbalances in dopamine have been implicated in a variety of mental disorders including schizophrenia, obsessive-compulsive disorder, drug addiction, and now ADHD.

Please understand that if a DNA or gene connection is made with ADD/ADHD (IA/HM), as it probably will be one day, that still doesn't mean it is a disease. It probably means we have found one component that contributes to the normal physiological differences of children labeled as ADD/ADHD (IA/HM) and nothing more. Eventually, we'll find these genetic components for just about every behavior pattern, including introversion and extroversion, anxiety, being a happy or sad person, being energetic or not energetic, active or less active, and so forth. Once again, none of these are diseases. DNA findings only explain the genes and our physiologies that underlie every form of normal behavior. Thus, we still have to deal with the issue of well-defined boundaries for disease versus nondisease.

One important argument against the genetic theories is the growth of 400 to 500 percent in the diagnosis of ADD/ADHD (IA/HM) since 1988. Genetic characteristics generally remain stable from one generation to the next. If they do increase, the increase will be slight, and not

400 or 500 percent. Such an increase argues more for social-familial changes, which have been very dramatic in the last twenty years, than for the genetic theories. We need also to consider that perhaps our children have been doing so poorly on educational measurements that there is a growing tendency to exert stronger controls over students' behavior. Even mild disruptions may interfere with a class's performance, and perhaps teachers are feeling pressured to subdue even mild disruptions in the learning environment. Or perhaps growing problems in our society are adding to the growth of disruptive students in the classroom, and more and more teachers are quickly flagging them. We'll examine the arguments for social and familial changes in chapter 4 to help explain this explosion of inattentive and highly misbehaving children. I see these arguments as more convincing than any of the disease theories.

Finding an underlying physiological component and finding a genetic component would only indicate that a child tends to be more active. We all know that some children are born active while others are born more docile. If an active child has parents who do not have good intuitive parenting skills, in a family where there are also environmental problems and stress, then conditions may be ripe for an ADHD (HM) pattern of behavior to emerge. In turn, if a child is born more docile, then poor parenting and environmental stresses may produce an ADD (IA) pattern of behavior.

Genetic findings may not be all that crucial because, as B. F. Skinner (1971) said, "There's nothing we can do about it." All we can do is alter the child's behavior by controlling the environmental conditions. Using the CSP for parenting, we can bring the problems of ADD/ADHD completely under control—*without drugs*—whether it's genetic or not.

In my research on the CSP, I used a questionnaire for parents that directly matched the *DSM-IV* requirements for ADD/ADHD. I administered the checklist three times: at the initial evaluation, after treatment was completed, and during a one-year follow-up contact with the parents. At the first session all the children fulfilled all the requirements to be labeled ADD/ADHD, but after treatment and at the last session, none of the children met the requirements, nor did they at a follow-up contact one year later. Was the disease cured? Where did it go? I hope that researchers measure to see if any of their so-called physiological signs are still present after CSP treatment. Such findings would be quite helpful.

Finding physiological components of behavior still doesn't justify giving amphetamines to children. Remember the Zager and Evans song "In the Year 2525"? It predicted that our behavior will be determined by the pill we take each day. Can we ever relinquish our souls, our free wills, to pills? If we continue our current course, that is exactly what we'll be doing to our children.

PSYCHOLOGICAL TESTS DO NOT DIAGNOSE A DISEASE

When I was a graduate student working on my doctorate, I was required to take a very bizarre mixture of courses. Some of them involved learning how to administer and interpret psychological tests. Other courses involved reviewing the literature about how invalid these very same tests were. I was thoroughly confused. There were so many different kinds of tests, such as projective personality tests, objective personality tests, intelligence quotient (IQ) tests, standard questionnaire tests, and achievement and educational tests. It was baffling.

Then I read an incredibly scholarly book by Walter Mischel (1968) called *Personality and Assessment*. Mischel carefully reviewed and sorted out the complexities of understanding what these tests could and could not do. Do these tests predict behavior? I learned that a crucial issue for use of these tests was how well they predict real behavior, which is called *criterion validity*. I learned that personality tests were about as valid as Ouija boards. They had little or no validity, meaning they couldn't predict how anyone would actually behave.

IQ, achievement, and educational tests were (and still are) fairly valid in predicting how well an individual would perform in an academic setting, that is, school. They didn't predict behavior or conduct. They only indicated how well one could perform academically.

I also learned that questionnaires are only structured interviews that ask specific questions about how we actually behave. They are substitute questions by the psychologist, merely asking the parents or teachers what they observe a child doing at home or at school. They are not tests.

I've included samples of the primary questionnaires, the Connors Scales. These are checklists of a teacher's or parent's observations, with arbitrary points assigned to each question. When the points from the observers add up to an arbitrary number, the child then receives the label of either ADD or ADHD. That's all there is to it. It's a label. *It doesn't indicate an underlying disease.*

PARENTS' OBSERVATIONS

Child Name:_____ Child Age:____ Child Sex:____ Parent Name:_____

Instructions: Read each item below carefully, and decide how much you think your child has been bothered by this problem during the past month.

Not at All	Just a Little	Pretty Much	Very Much	CPRS-48
0	1	2	3	1. Picks at things (nails, fingers, hair, clothing)
0	1	2	3	2. Sassy to grown-ups
0	1	2	3	3. Excitable, impulsive
0	1	2	3	4. Sucks or chews (thumb, clothing, blankets)
0	1	2	3	5. Daydreams
0	1	2	3	6. Difficulty in learning

Child Name:_____ Child Age:____ Child Sex:____ Parent Name:_____

Instructions: Read each item below carefully, and decide how much you think your child has been bothered by this problem during the past month.

Not at All	Just a Little	Pretty Much	Very Much	CTRS-39
				CLASSROOM BEHAVIOR
0	1	2	3	1. Constantly fidgeting
0	1	2	3	2. Hums and makes other odd noises
0	1	2	3	3. Restless or overactive
0	1	2	3	4. Inattentive, easily distracted
0	1	2	3	5. Fails to finish things s/he starts—short attention span
0	1	2	3	6. Daydreams

TEACHER'S OBSERVATIONS

Child Name:_____ Child Age:____ Child Sex:____ Teacher Name:_____

Instructions: Read each item below carefully, and decide how much you think your child has been bothered by this problem during the past month.

Not at All	Just a Little	Pretty Much	Very Much	CTRS-28
0	1	2	3	1. Restless in the "squirmy" sense
0	1	2	3	2. Makes inappropriate noises when s/he shouldn't
0	1	2	3	3. Distractibility or attention span a problem
0	1	2	3	4. Disturbs other children
0	1	2	3	5. Daydreams
0	1	2	3	6. Restless, always up and on the go

If a child scores positive for ADD/ADHD, that only means he has accumulated enough points to be *called* ADD/ADHD. It does not mean a child *has* ADD/ADHD. With the labels IA/HM, I hope this perception changes.

Oddly, I find that even psychologists, psychiatrists, and educators fail to understand this concept. When a child gets enough points and a label, professionals also mistakenly believe they've uncovered a disease. When they tell a parent their child *has* ADD/ADHD, they honestly believe in what they are saying. But it's just not accurate—it's only a label and not proof of a disease.

Whenever possible, the behaviorists prefer direct observation of a child to determine if he or she is inattentive (IA) or highly misbehaving (HM). To them, questionnaires are only a substitute for getting out in the field, or real world, in order to actually observe. While this increases the accuracy of labels, it does not support the inference of a disease.

I hope this chapter clarifies the issues about there being no disease. There may be underlying physiological patterns for ADD/ADHD (IA/HM), but these only reflect normal patterns of more active children. There may be a genetic component to these normal physiological patterns; and psychological tests are substitute observations for labeling, and not for indicating that a child has a disease.

The next chapter focuses on the familial and social problems that may truly underlie the explosion in the diagnosing of ADD/ADHD (IA/HM).

CHAPTER 4

Modern Family and Social Problems That Underlie the ADD/ADHD (IA/HM) Explosion

R ECALL, IF YOU WILL, our discussion about the almost 500 percent increase in children diagnosed as ADD/ADHD (IA/HM) since 1989. Are there other possible causes than the neurobiological and disease theories that can explain this phenomenon?

If we present normal children who may have a biological

predisposition at birth for being more active with some of the social problems facing American families today, then we have the perfect setting for the development of all types of childhood problems, including ADD/ADHD (IA/HM). Notice I said "predisposition for being more active." Indeed, we all know that some children are more active at birth, but we also know they are within normal limits. Add years of environmental and family stresses to this predisposition, and we increase the risk that children will develop problems. Could some of these problems be caused by a lack of motivation to do well in school? Yes. Could some of these problems be a desire to test authority figures and frequently misbehave? Yes. Could some of these problems take the form of reckless and nonthinking behavior? Yes.

This chapter will explore some of the family and social problems besetting children today. These problems contribute far more to the epidemic explosion of ADD/ADHD (IA/HM) diagnoses than does the biological makeup of these children.

WHAT IS ADD/ADHD?

I suspect that most of you reading this book have been over the diagnostic criteria countless times. But for the sake of readers who haven't, I've included the *DSM-IV* criteria in Table 4.1.

You'll notice that ADD children don't have many of the behavioral problems listed: They just don't pay attention to their schoolwork. That's why I prefer to call them Inattentive or IA. The problem is cognitive, concerned with thoughts, beliefs, and motivation. They won't pay

TABLE 4. 1

Diagnostic and Statistical Manual–IV for Psychiatry and Psychology Criteria for Attention Deficit/Hyperactivity Disorder

Either (1) or (2):

(1) six (or more) of the following symptoms of **inattention** have persisted for at least six months to a degree that is maladaptive and inconsistent with developmental level:

INATTENTION

(a) often fails to give close attention to details or makes careless mistakes in schoolwork, work, or other activities

(b) often has difficulty sustaining attention in tasks or play activities

(c) often does not seem to listen when spoken to directly

(d) often does not follow through on instructions and fails to finish schoolwork, chores, or duties in the workplace (not due to oppositional behavior or failure to understand instructions)

(e) often has difficulty organizing tasks and activities

(f) often avoids, dislikes, or is reluctant to engage in tasks that require sustained mental effort (such as schoolwork or homework)

(g) often loses things necessary for tasks or activities (e.g., toys, school assignments, pencils, books, or tools)

(h) is often easily distracted by extraneous stimuli

(i) is often forgetful in daily activities

(2) six (or more) of the following symptoms of **hyperactivity-impulsivity** have persisted for at least six months to a degree that is maladaptive and inconsistent with developmental level:

HYPERACTIVITY

(a) often fidgets with hands or feet or squirms in seat

(b) often leaves seat in classroom or in other situations in which remaining seated is expected

(c) often runs about or climbs excessively in situations in which it is inappropriate (in adolescents or adults may be limited to subjective feelings or restlessness)

(d) often has difficulty playing or engaging in leisure activities quietly

(e) is often "on the go" or often acts as if "driven by a motor"

(f) often talks excessively

IMPULSIVITY

(g) often blurts out answers before questions have been completed

(h) often has difficulty awaiting turn; often interrupts or intrudes on others (e.g., butts into conversations or games)

---

attention to activities they don't like, which is most often schoolwork, and they will pay attention to activities they like, such as TV or video games. Russell Barkley has repeatedly attributed this selectivity of attention to some mysterious disease. I attribute it to a selectivity or a lack of motivation. They hate school and, therefore, they won't pay attention. They like TV and, therefore, they'll attend for hours. This makes more sense to me than some mysteriously highly selective disease no one can find.

The primary characteristics of ADD/ADHD children are that they don't pay attention *and* they misbehave a lot. The disease theorists claim they can't control themselves unless they have drugs. After over twenty years of successfully working with these children, I know they indeed can behave, they can control themselves, and they can pay attention when they are supposed to—all without drugs.

One of the most important lessons we have learned in psychology in the last thirty years is that behaviors result from cognitive (thinking or belief) patterns. To effectively change the problem behaviors of ADD/ADHD children it is essential to understand their underlying cognitions. The three basic cognitive patterns are:

1. They simply DO NOT THINK.
2. They hate schoolwork.
3. They are shortsighted and do not consider long-term goals important.

It was Phil Kendall (1996) who repeatedly emphasized that the primary problem of ADD/ADHD is *not thinking*. This means that they do not attend to their behavior; they don't pay attention to the rules; they don't monitor what they are doing; they barge full steam ahead at doing things without thinking. Additional cognitive patterns include *hating schoolwork and shortsightedness*. Notice I said hating schoolwork, and not hating school. Some ADD/ADHD enjoy attending school and being with friends, but almost without exception they hate schoolwork. To them schoolwork is boring drudgery, for which they will exert only minimal effort in order to get the work hastily finished. This explains why their work is often incomplete and sloppy. Often, ADD/ADHD are diagnosed as having a *comorbid "disease" called agraphia*, or poor handwriting. Agraphia is designated in the *DSM-IV* as a learning disability. As John Rosemond says, this is another example of psychobabble. To me, it is amazing how this so-called "disease" also disappears when their ADD/ADHD behaviors are brought under control. When they are required to pay attention and complete their schoolwork more carefully, their handwriting magically becomes "normal."

Our job in the CSP is not merely to get their behavior

under control but to train them to pay attention, to be aware of what they are doing, and to appreciate the impact of their behaviors on others around them at all times—in other words, to train them to start *actively thinking*. There are additional steps parents can take to help ADD/ADHD children to actually love learning and develop a goal-oriented, strong sense of purpose for their lives.

One of the interesting features of the *DSM-IV* criteria for ADD/ADHD (IA/HM) is that the constellation of inattentiveness and misbehaviors that are listed occurs mostly at school. I don't know of any writer or researcher who has ever picked up on this pattern. A major component of the CSP is to switch the focus from working with these children initially in school to the home. We first work on the set of misbehaviors that occurs within the family or home setting, where parents can exert so much more control over them. Once these children are stabilized at home, school problems automatically disappear in about 80 percent of them. In the remaining 20 percent, additional work will then be necessary to get these children to pay attention, behave properly, and do their work diligently in school.

What are the social and family problems that are adding to the growing rate of children who are IA (ADD) and HM (ADHD)?

THE HASSLED, HARRIED, AND OVERLOADED AMERICAN FAMILY

I recall that back in the '60s in my psychology courses there were predictions that the task of future psychologists would be helping people deal with excessive leisure time. It didn't quite work out that way, did it?

Social and economic changes have required the American family to deal with an almost overwhelming daily stressful schedule. Consider that for the majority of two-parent households both partners must work to make ends meet. Financial and daily stress difficulties are even far greater for single parents, who now compose over 50 percent of American households. The daily rush begins in the wee morning hours, around six A.M. Have coffee, get the kids up, get them fed, leave them alone to catch the school bus because you have to get to your job, or drive the little ones to day care, fight traffic, and then work at your stressful job all day. After work, it's fight traffic again, pick up the little ones from day care, and then return to a house that looks as if a cyclone ripped through it. Prepare dinner, eat (usually in front of the TV), clean the kitchen, run around the house spot-cleaning and picking up loose clothing from the floor, help the children with homework, get them bathed, and hopefully get them tucked in at bedtime. Weekends are little better. They are usually filled with a flurry of required chores, such as grocery shopping, doing laundry, housecleaning, working in the yard, cleaning the cars, buying needed clothing or other necessities, and on and on. I get tired just writing this list.

How can children get their needs met for love, attention, nurturance, and guidance with this frantic lifestyle? Writer Thomas Moore in his book *Care of the Soul* (1992) calls this "The Modernist Syndrome." He states that these conditions are ripe for us and our children to develop all kinds of emotional, behavioral, and psychological problems, ADD/ADHD (IA/HM) included.

In almost all my writings, I talk about De Jure and De Facto Neglect of children. De Jure is severe, characterized by lack of food or clothing, where legal authorities can step in to protect a child. De Facto is unintended and often unnoticed neglect of our children's needs for lots of love and attention. Too many of our children are victims of this pattern. How can they develop solid values, emotional stability, behavioral self-control, and a strong drive or motivation to do well if there is no one there to teach and instill these things within them? Later we'll discuss some possible solutions.

Please don't feel guilty. The social and economic conditions that created this way of life were beyond your or my control. But there are things we can do to possibly get some parts of our lives under control and be able to care for our children more effectively.

Timothy

Timothy was eight years old when I first saw him. The school guidance counselor had referred him. At the initial intake interview, his parents said the school psychologist had evaluated him and diagnosed Timothy as ADHD. In school, he rarely completed assignments, often played with pens pretending they were rocket ships, called out frequently, pushed in line, did his work in a sloppy fashion, and often talked to nearby children during lessons. When reprimanded by the teacher, he would immediately comply, only to misbehave again five minutes later.

At home his parents had to repeat commands several times until he complied; he had daily episodes of temper tantrums; he whined and cried frequently when he didn't get his way; he would not do his homework unless a parent sat with him; he constantly fought with his sister; he left a mess throughout the house, and on and on. His parents yelled at Timothy several times each day and spanked him three to five times per week.

Both of Timothy's parents worked. He was left alone each morning to lock up the house and go alone to the school bus stop. After school, he met the day-care van and stayed at day care until six P.M., when one parent would pick him up. When he got home, the daily ritual dictated that he have dinner in his room while watching TV. His parents ate their dinner in the family room while watching the news. He'd usually finish his homework either in school or at the day care, and of course it was usually incomplete and sloppy. After dinner, Timothy either watched TV or played video games in his room. Often he'd wander around the house getting into trouble with his sister and his parents. Timothy's dad usually spent the evenings doing paperwork from his office or watching TV. His mother cleaned up around the house. A battle usually ensued at bedtime to get him to bathe and go to sleep.

Weekends for Timothy were spent in front of the TV or playing outside with neighborhood kids. His parents usually were busy with household chores. The family did not attend church.

Looking at the case of Timothy, we can clearly see an overall pattern of De Facto Neglect. After his parents were made aware of what was happening, and after being trained in the CSP, all these routines changed. His parents were plainly unaware of their neglect of him. They got Timothy under control and deliberately changed their routines to give him the love, time, and attention he desperately needed. The case ended well.

Moving

When I give talks and mention the word *moving*, audiences often scoff at first. But as I develop my points they listen.

Did you know that 20 percent of families in the United States move each year? The U. S. Postal Service reports that forty million families move from city to city each year.

Corporations require moving, especially for promotions. It's also required by the military, and it's often necessary to finishing college and graduate school training. On my street, four houses have sold this year alone. Each household had young children.

What impact does moving have on children? Indeed, the loss of familiar surroundings, friends, and their school is tremendously difficult for them. Then, once they're relocated, imagine what it is like to be "the new kid on the block." It is so hard for children to make new friends.

The repeated losses that result from moving dampen children's motivation. Why try when everything keeps getting ripped out from under them? Why care about anything if they keep losing it? It hurts too much to sustain such losses.

The emotional turmoil from the upheaval of moving may take the form of disruptive behaviors, just to get attention. It may take the form of not attending to their work because it's so defeating to start to prove oneself all over again in a new school. How can children function and concentrate when they are nervous from such upheavals in their lives?

But there's a more powerful problem with moving that dramatically contributes to the creation of the ADD/ADHD (IA/HM) child: loss of their extended family.

LOSS OF THE EXTENDED FAMILY

The extended family formed the foundation of family life in this country until around 1970. Sociologists describe the extended kinship family as consisting of grandma, grandpa, aunts, uncles, and cousins. They lived close to one another. They may have argued with one another, but there was deep love. Family members were there for support and help in times of tribulation. But, of particular importance, devotion and love for the children was central to the families' attentions.

Children were the hope of the family. Future generations were viewed as the vehicles for a better life. The extended family was a powerful force in which children developed values to succeed, get ahead, and help raise the socioeconomic level of the family to higher levels. Children who grew up in such surroundings became powerfully motivated to do well in school. For most families, education was seen as the primary vehicle for upward mobility and hope for the future. Children took school seriously. From all family members, deep values were instilled to succeed. *Children who develop these deep values do not become ADD/ADHD.*

Other important values were learned through the larger family. Most family members also repeatedly instilled honesty, integrity, sharing, and helping. A child was surrounded by an ample supply of role models who provided and encouraged children to adopt these strong values and beliefs. Moving has spread families far and wide, and now the extended family is almost extinct.

Since this form of family life disappeared from the American scene largely due to increased mobility, a primary mechanism for teaching children deep values has gone. Is it any wonder that without this family structure surrounding children we're seeing the explosion in the diagnosis of ADD/ADHD (IA/HM)? Do you realize what this does to children?

Today children have neither their immediate family nor their extended family. Where are the sources from which they can learn the deep values of "stick-to-itiveness," hard work, and love of education? If these values are not deeply rooted, then why should children like school? Why should they pay attention? Why should they honor authority figures? Why should they control their behavior? These values, imparted by the immediate and extended family, underlie behaviors. Without these values, there are no constraints on behavior. A child is a lost and aimless wanderer. Then we make our children take drugs to fix the problem.

DIVORCE

We can't ignore the contribution that divorce makes toward the gigantic escalation in children being labeled ADD/ADHD (IA/HM). The divorce rate is currently approaching the 67 percent mark, and single parents are raising 50 percent of all children.

I realize that many of you reading this already feel terrible about the impact of a broken marriage on your children. It's not my intention to inflict wounds on anyone. I'm divorced. Divorce is a harsh reality. We can't deny its impact on children.

The same stresses or daily hassles I mentioned earlier are perhaps the single greatest cause of broken homes. It's difficult for couples to stay together when they are constantly tired and overwhelmed. Frustrations develop into being "edgy," which is often expressed as anger with those immediately around us. Being exhausted doesn't quite contribute to feeling affectionate or sexy. When chores are left uncompleted, we sometimes think the other person isn't doing his or her share. Resentments build, tensions mount, and tempers flare until, after several years, the bonds snap. Sadly, it is the children who pay the dearest price.

Often battles ensue after a breakup. The air is thick with tension. The tension probably has been there for years, but after the break it usually gets even worse. Sometimes parents enter legal battles that children witness. Their hearts are torn when they see the two people they love and rely on going at each other. Under those conditions, a child's spirit breaks. He stops caring. Work and school aren't worth the trouble, since to him life is so bleak anyway. Then we call him ADD/ADHD (IA/HM).

Visitations are hard on children. There's little sense of stability. Often they go from a house with one style of parenting and one set of rules to another house where everything is very different. When I train divorced parents in CSP, I diligently try to get both parents to attend the sessions so they can provide a consistently structured environment for their child. Fighting over how to parent stops after they both complete the training.

Parents: Both of you read this book. If you love your

child, and I know you do, put his or her needs ahead of any issues that lie between you. Set your differences aside. Learn how both of you can take care of your child in a healthy and loving way. The answers lie between the covers of this book. Work together as a team for the sake of your most precious God-given gift.

Single parents have a particularly difficult problem with parenting. If you felt stressed when there were two of you, quadruple the feeling for the single parent. What you learn here will bring your child under control and help make your lives easier. It will actually bring you closer together.

Sherry and Lynn

I used to teach the CSP to groups of fifteen families at a time for eight-week blocks of time. Many single parents went though the classes. Two mothers, Sherry and Lynn, both had nightmarish ADHD (HM) children, and they both had enormous financial problems. Neither had time for a social life. Things were tough, indeed.

Without my knowledge, the two of them went for coffee after each class and became friends. They developed a marvelous solution to their dilemma.

They sold their separate houses and bought a larger one, sharing lowered mortgage payments and other reduced expenses. They both carried out the CSP with great diligence. They exchanged weekends in which one of them would be free to date or be with friends while the other took care of the children. In other words, they solved many of their problems.

For several years I periodically heard from them that the arrangement was going extremely well. Most important, with both mothers using the CSP the children bene-fited—all ADHD (HM) behaviors ceased and academic performance improved considerably.

MEDIA

Children spend on average over five hours a day watching TV. Many come home to empty houses after school, with no one there to supervise them. Where do they go imme-diately? Right to the TV.

What do our children watch? Consider the distorted, perverse values they learn from the media. It's not just the excessive content of sex and violence that is disturbing. Many shows infuse messages of contempt for education. It's cool to hate school. Shows often portray role models who are rebellious toward authority figures. Cursing is dis-played as everyday, acceptable language.

Some children are more malleable and suggestible than others, more prone to adopt the values they witness from the media. This, too, can be a major contributor to loss of moti-vation and can increase lack of respect for rules and author-ity. The media may be significantly contributing to the mas-sive escalation of children being labeled ADD/ADHD.

Are you beginning to understand that children's values and motivation are a major force in how they behave? I see ADD/ADHD (IA/HM) not as a disease of the body, but more as a *disease of modern society*. In chapter 13 we'll go into some important values to teach children and how to help them avoid the onset of attentional problems or eliminate them. We will talk about how to fill children's time con-structively and reduce their exposure to trash media.

There are some excellent quality shows. There are educational and entertaining shows that can amply fill some of the time they spend watching TV. Think and plan what you let them watch.

PEERS

You may be the most perfect parent in the world, but the parents of children with whom your child associates may not be. The values of other children can be a strong influence on the values your child develops. If your child's friends are antischool and have no respect for authority, then your child may become that way too. Later in this chapter I'll offer some potential solutions for helping your child develop friendships that exert a more positive influence.

SOLUTIONS

In this section we are going to explore some prospective solutions to the problems that beset families. You can accept or reject these suggestions at will. They are suggestions, not mandates.

PARENTING

Some people have better intuition about parenting skills than others. But consider the four most fundamental areas of our lives: parenting our children, being married, taking care of our own emotional selves, and performing our jobs.

Notice that only in one area do most of us receive instruction—in performing our jobs. The other three are left to intuition and, judging from the statistics, we don't have particularly good batting averages.

If your child is ADD/ADHD (IA/HM), then you need help in learning how to parent her. That is what this book is all about. You'll learn every element that you'll need to parent your child and eliminate the problem behaviors and poor thinking patterns associated with ADD/ADHD (IA/HM).

Thus your first step is to learn the CSP, beginning in the next chapter, and take command of the situation.

TIME AND COMMUNICATION

Bonding with your child is crucial. If you have a close, mutually loving relationship with him or her, you have considerable influence over your child.

Once you get your child under control with the CSP, the stress in your life will be considerably reduced; then you will actually enjoy being able to give your child the time and attention he or she needs. Developing a close, loving, and enjoyable relationship with your child is an integral part of the philosophy of the CSP.

1. Get up fifteen or twenty minutes earlier in the morning, and get your child up earlier too. "What?" you say. Believe me, it's worth it because it enables you and your child to have breakfast together. Start the day on a family note. Make breakfast a warm and caring way to start each day. Whatever you do, "Don't teach and don't preach."

Talk about fun things. Ask him what's ahead for the day. Talk about projects he's working on. Show an interest in his life. Share some of the things that are exciting and important to you, but don't dominate. The most basic rule is to *listen*.

Joke with him, kid around, and have fun at the breakfast table. Start his day by avoiding the typical helter-skelter pattern you've been following. It's unnerving to everybody, and it doesn't help with your relationship.

2. Have dinner together when everyone returns home. Avoid eating dinner in front of the TV, as a growing number of American families are doing. Once again, talk about the day. Joke and have fun. Listen—don't preach. Work on bonding. Teaching your child values should be done by patient coaxing and nudging. By growing close as a family, he'll be far more receptive to learning from you.

   Require him to help with cleanup after dinner. The CSP will teach you how to accomplish this without World War III erupting. This should be a nightly routine. It is a good way to help him learn responsibility and sharing. If you kid and joke around, this can be a very positive time for all of you.

3. Spend one hour each night reading together as a family. Stop being hypnotized by the TV, and turn it off. Your child needs to see you read if she is going to value reading. My boys are thirteen and fourteen. When we read together, you can hear a pin drop. We've been doing this since they first began reading. It is a time of closeness that has always given me a wonderful feeling of joy.

4. At bedtime sit and talk to your child individually, for ten or fifteen minutes. Pull a chair next to the bed and just talk. Try to keep conversations soft in tone and light in content. The relationship exceeds the importance of any lessons you may want to drive home to him. By growing close, you will have more influence over him when it really counts. By growing close, he will *want* to learn from you. Be patient, and remember that this process takes more than twenty-one years.

5. Make your worship day, whether it be Saturday or Sunday, your day to rest and be together. Try to get all your chores and responsibilities completed and be totally free on worship day. It can be hard, but it is possible. I think of worship day as a quiet, family-oriented day. An occasional activity is OK—but strive for serenity.

I like using the slow cooker on Sunday so that after church we return home to a wonderful meal. Make this meal leisurely, very leisurely. After you eat, go for a long walk together. Deepak Chopra talks about how quiet walks are a way to combine a form of meditation and exercise. Walks can also be great times for family closeness.

If your child is amenable, hold hands. Sadly, my guys are too big for that now, and I miss it.

When you return home, read, play a board game, nap, watch a fire—just be close! Remembering these warm, wonderful days will remain important to your child throughout his lifetime. Build such memories.

Days like this are therapeutic for you too. You need the rest. It is a good way to build family life and spiritual values at the same time. This part of American life has been disappearing for over thirty years, but as parents we can salvage it.

6. If you are a two-parent family, take a hard look at your budget, and see if one of you can quit work. Don't go ballistic—give me a chance. If both of you are dedicated to careers, this may not be a likely option. But if one of you has a job you're not particularly crazy about, it may surprise you to learn that you might be better off financially by actually quitting. Family financial consultants are teaching how we can do this and actually come out ahead. Perhaps there is a way for one of you to have more time with the children.

Try the following exercise:

A. In detail, list the automobile expenses related to your job. Include:
   (1) gasoline expenses to and from work
   (2) tolls
   (3) loss to the value of your car because of higher mileage
   (4) expenses for car repairs because of stop-and-go mileage to and from work
   (5) parking fees
   (6) if public transportation is used, list weekly or monthly fares
B. How much money do you spend for clothing related to your job?
C. What are the extra food expenses because of working?
   (1) Do you frequently purchase fast foods for dinner because of your hectic schedule? How much do

you spend? How much would you save if you were to stay home and carefully plan budget meals (which are probably healthier)?

(2) Do you buy lunch out as opposed to eating a simple meal at home?

(3) How much can you save on your grocery bills if you clip coupons? I know families that reduce their grocery bills by $25.00 or more each week.

D. How much does day care cost you? Where I live, the average day-care facility charges between $80.00 and $100.00 per week per child. It's usually $150.00 for infant care. This is an enormous amount of money. Think about the number of hours your children spend at day-care centers. How much more time will they have at home with you if you're not working?

E. Can you provide day care for a few children at your home?

(1) If you charged $80.00 per week per child for four children you would be providing more personal care for these children and earning $320.00 per week gross income.

(2) By providing day care you can earn tax deductions for:

(a) related food expenses

(b) depreciation on your mortgage payments equal to the percentage of space you use for day-care purposes

(c) deductions for play equipment (both indoor and outdoor) and toys

(d) depreciation for use of your car for day-care purposes

(e) food purchases for day care

F. If providing child care is not appealing, consider other types of at-home jobs, such as working for computer-based Web companies, for example.

G. Can your spouse come home for lunch? If he or she can, you can save restaurant expenses and perhaps have a little extra time together.

H. How many workdays does it cost you to be absent from work when the children are sick?

It can be scary to give up the cash flow you're used to. But you may actually earn more money by following these suggestions.

Perhaps there are other hidden benefits. Ask yourself if staying home would reduce the daily stresses for you, your spouse, and your children. You may have more time and less rushing for car repairs, shopping, housecleaning, and other chores. *Can the turmoil in your household be considerably reduced?*

Let's get back to more solutions.

7. I find that organized sports and activities can increase the stresses on children. Are your children on teams? How many? How often do they practice and have games? Do your children take music lessons? Are they members of Boy Scouts or Girl Scouts? What about karate lessons? Are they in other organized activities? How much time does this consume each week? How stressful is it for you and the children to rush to each activity?

Perhaps you can handle only one organized activity each season. I think that a calmer and less over-scheduled lifestyle is important in calming down

ADD/ADHD (IA/HM) children. Overstimulation keeps them in a constant state of agitation. A calm environment helps make them less anxious and stressed.

8. With how many community and church commitments are you involved? Many of us feel it is important to give a fair portion of our time and energy to helping others, participating in community organizations such as Lions, Rotary, Junior League, and church activities. But consider whether this heightens your stresses and detracts from essential time with your children.

I've known several families that were deeply committed to church activities, such as helping to feed the homeless and visiting the elderly, but didn't realize how extensive the church schedule was, or how it detracted from time with their own children.

9. Recall our discussion on the detrimental effects of moving. An article in *USA Today* stated that a growing number of corporate executives are declining promotions because of the requirement to move. They feel that such moves are too disruptive to the lives of their children, and they have chosen family over career. Perhaps corporate leaders will realize what their moving policies are doing to families and to the country. Perhaps they will change company policy and promote employees without making it necessary to move far, by letting them move within a region.

Holding the extended family together is essential if we're going to reinstate the most important source for elevating the moral climate of America. I'll bet that if we could rebuild the extended family and stabilize children's lives, we'd begin to see a reduction in the number of children diagnosed as ADD/ADHD (IA/HM). This can happen faster if long distance moving is reduced or eliminated.

10. Take time for family activities. I know how busy your lives are, but perhaps once a month you can do something together—all of you. Think about camping, fishing, and hiking. Think about educational excursions to museums, historical sites, college campuses, or sporting events. I'm sure you can think of a wide variety of fun things to do. Not only do these activities help you in bonding with your children, but they also help excite children's interest in learning new things about history and nature.

11. Perhaps one of the most important things you can do to bond with your child and prevent ADD/ADHD (IA/HM) is simply to have FUN.

Alex

A few weeks ago my son Alex and I were home alone. Kevin was having alone time with his mom. Even though we're divorced, we periodically deliberately exchange alone times with the children to help foster closeness. One evening, for some strange reason, Alex and I looked at each other and began laughing. The more we laughed, the more we lost control. After twenty minutes of sidesplitting silliness, we were able to get somewhat under control. Alex, who loves magic tricks, asked if I wanted to see him balance an upside-down glass of water on his head. I said sure. He walked over with the glass on his head, and I jumped up, scaring him. The water spilled all over him. We broke out laughing for another twenty minutes.

When we began to calm down, I told him to bring me a glass of water and I'd show him how to perform the trick correctly. He did. I took the glass and dumped the water on his head. We lost it for almost an hour. I kept saying jokingly, "Son, I can't believe you were dumb enough to hand me the water." We laughed uncontrollably some more. Suddenly, I looked up as a giant thirty-two-ounce cup of water came down on me. We laughed more.

Both boys have a devilish sense of humor. Times like these bring us closer. As you grow closer in such crazy, fun ways, your influence over your children grows. They will want to learn from you. They will want to please you. They will want to adopt your values. Your approval for their hard efforts will take on new importance, and they'll work hard and not become ADD/ADHD (IA/HM). Motivated children who come from close parental bonding don't become ADD/ADHD. The CSP is a firm model for parenting, but it's equally as important to have fun. A good rule to remember when learning the CSP is to "Be firm—be fun."

PEERS

Help your child develop friendships with children who come from good families and reflect healthy values. The issue of healthy peer relations becomes more and more crucial as your child approaches the teen years. Where teens are concerned, I often state that "Who their friends are is who children will become." Begin the process of engineering with whom your child socializes early in his life. Your place of worship is probably the optimal choice for fellowship and socialization. Does your place of worship have active child and adolescent programs? If so, check out the program, and if your impression is positive, get your child actively involved. Community centers and Boy/Girl Scouts are also worthy of consideration. Observe, evaluate, and get to know the other parents before making a commitment. It's a good idea not to leave the selection of your child's friends to chance, but to deliberately design it, steering him in a healthy direction before the teen years arrive.

Consider some of these suggestions. The CSP will get them under control, but these changes are equally important. Grow close. Work on their values. Influence them with patience and love.

EDUCATION AND POLITICS

I've been an educator for almost thirty years. ADD/ADHD is predominantly an education- and school-related problem. The *DSM-IV* diagnosis criteria are based mostly on school behaviors, such as pushing in line, calling out without raising a hand, fidgeting in a seat, and so on. The explosion of the label ADD/ADHD is the product of the simple truth that these children hate school. Are the schools contributing to the 500 percent increase in this problem over the last ten years? I believe the answer is yes, and I believe that well-meaning politicians are contributing to this problem.

Politicians are constantly campaigning on the cliché-based platform of "Back to basics." They frequently point out that American children score poorly in reading, math, and science compared to children from other countries, such as Japan and Germany. Increasingly, they are passing state laws establishing systems of SOL (Standards of Learning) tests as means of improving curricula and school performance. I like SOLs, but as they are currently enforced they are contributing to the growth of kids' being labeled as ADD/ADHD and to the escalation of education problems.

Several consequences have emerged from these political philosophies:

1. *All* schoolchildren are being treated as candidates for college. As a result, curricula are designed strictly for college preparation. Heavy emphasis is placed on strict adherence to pure academics. Fun and creativity-developing activities such as art, music, or even free play are being reduced or completely removed. The needs of noncollege-bound students are not being met. These are the children who want to work with their hands, and who want to develop more pragmatic skills, such as putting things together or fixing things. To them, schoolwork has become increasingly arduous, meaningless, and boring. They are made to sit still throughout an academic day, being required to focus their attention on material they hate. Is it any wonder that many of these children won't sit still or pay attention? Then we label them as sick and fill them with pills to restrain their restlessness. My state, Virginia, since the SOLs have gotten poor results, is now considering a separate system of SOLs, for the college-bound and the noncollege-bound.

2. Academic material that used to be introduced in the second and third grades is now part of the kindergarten curriculum. Immediately children are started

on reading and math. Fun activities, such as playing musical instruments, dancing, and free play have increasingly been reduced. By the time these children reach third grade they are burned out. School becomes boring and arduous. They resent the excessive emphasis on academics. This orientation also contributes to more and more children hating schoolwork. Oddly, those countries scoring higher academically have retained the more fun and relaxed curricula.

3. Time for free play and physical education has been decreased. Children are made to sit still in uncomfortable seats for long hours, with less and less opportunity to exercise and burn off energy. Boys are diagnosed as ADD/ADHD at five times the rate of girls. Is it possibly because they have less padding on their bottoms and find it harder to sit in uncomfortable seats for long hours? Did you know that in many states school furniture is made in the prisons? Are the prisoners getting back at us through our children?

4. I teach in a state college. Professors are increasingly upset that many entering students are simply poor college material. Attending a state institution is like having a scholarship, because tuition is supplemented by state tax dollars. Why are we helping pay for the education of marginal students? Each year more and more students are bringing disability notes to me claiming that they are ADD/ADHD, and therefore, because they are "handicapped," I'm required to provide special conditions for their taking tests and for their note taking during lecture. Why can't politicians run on a platform to reduce the size of state campuses, provide education for students based on a combined

formula of financial need and excellence in scholarship, and lessen the tax dollars spent on students who aren't learning or can't learn at the college level? Why must every student in a given state have a right to a college education supported with tax money? Wouldn't the voters be happier with the savings of tax money being passed on as reductions in taxes? Politicians can garner votes on this new platform.

It is less expensive to supplement vocational programs at community or junior colleges. Then both students and taxpayers would be happy. No research has been done on this yet, but I'll bet that fewer students would declare themselves as ADD/ADHD in college if they could pursue studies that they liked more and for which they were better suited. If students wish to change to a more academically focused program, the community colleges could easily provide for such a switch.

Did you know that ADD/ADHD was not included in the original Americans with Disabilities Act? It was added only after being demanded by an irate parents' group called CHADD (Children with Attention Deficit Disorder).

To me learning and education are sacred. If we make our school curricula fun, explorative, less pressured, and more relaxed, we will see fewer children who hate schoolwork and fewer children labeled as ADD/ADHD. Pills can't fix this problem; parents and voters can.

In the next chapter I'll begin your journey to learn how to *stop* ADD/ADHD (IA/HM). We'll start learning the Caregivers' Skills Program (CSP).

CHAPTER 5

The Big Change
in Parenting

THE PARENTING PROGRAMS that are currently available aren't working well. In this chapter we'll not only explore why these approaches aren't working but see how they actually worsen the problems of ADD/ADHD (IA/HM). On the surface, they seem to be sensible, but as we examine more closely we'll see that they contribute to the underlying thinking or cognitive patterns of ADD/ADHD (IA/HM). By making matters worse, current programs are perpetuating the ADD/ADHD (IA/HM) problems into adolescence and even adulthood, and thus often necessitating that the use of drugs continues for more and more years.

We'll look at a very different technique—the Caregivers' Skills Program (CSP), which is designed not only to stop the ADD/ADHD (IA/HM) behaviors but also to stop the ADD/ADHD (IA/HM) thinking problems. The CSP works. It will train your child to behave and think more satisfactorily and no longer need any drugs.

THE BIG CHANGE

I want specifically to point out why current programs aren't working and why they make matters worse. In order to do this, I have to teach you a very basic behavioral concept. Note the model below:

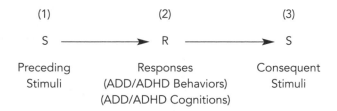

(1)	(2)	(3)
S ⟶	R ⟶	S
Preceding Stimuli	Responses (ADD/ADHD Behaviors) (ADD/ADHD Cognitions)	Consequent Stimuli

This model represents how we behave and think. In psychology it's called *operant condition*, which was introduced by B. F. Skinner in the 1930s. It's a very basic model for behavior modification.

The first S, at point 1, stands for preceding stimuli. These are the events that happen before a behavior, such as a traffic light turning red. They provide cues or prompts that tell us what we are supposed to do next. The red traffic light tells us to put our foot on the brake pedal and stop the car. Telling Johnny to "Be quiet!" is a preceding stimulus that tells him to stop talking. Shortly, we're going to learn how current behavioral approaches place most of their emphasis on what parents and teachers do that precedes the ADD/ADHD (IA/HM) child's behavior and why those approaches work only if the child is on drugs. Without the drugs, those programs don't work.

The R, at point 2, stands for responses. These are the behaviors and cognitions (thoughts) that compose the patterns we call ADD/ADHD (IA/HM). Typically the *behaviors* consist of such things as being impulsive, calling out, pushing other children, interrupting, and all the other actions listed in Table 4.1. The R also stands for the *thinking and cognitive* patterns that underlie ADD/ADHD (IA/HM), the most important of which is *"Not Thinking."* Not thinking means that ADD/ADHD (IA/HM) children don't pay attention to the people around them, they don't think about how they are behaving, and they don't think about the impact or consequences of their behaviors on others. This not thinking results in an inattentive (IA), highly misbehaving (HM), and obnoxious child. Other programs actually reinforce, perpetuate, and make worse the Not Thinking pattern. Other programs are not designed to alter this thinking problem in any way, and, therefore, they don't work well.

The S, at point 3, stands for consequent stimuli. They are the consequences, consisting of rewards and punishments, that occur after the behaviors. Current programs actually reinforce the very ADD/ADHD (IA/HM) behaviors and nonthinking patterns we're trying to get rid of. In the CSP you'll learn the step-by-step things you'll need to know to stop the entire ADD/ADHD (IA/HM) pattern. The greater part of this book is devoted to comprehensively teaching the entire "nuts and bolts" of how to erase and reverse your child's problems.

THE ERRORS OF CURRENT PARENTING APPROACHES

Current parenting programs for ADD/ADHD (IA/HM) children do control behaviors. But there are two major problems: First, they rely on the amphetamine drugs, and, second, they make the child highly dependent on constant assistance and help. Overall, they increasingly handicap the child. Then when the drugs are stopped, in most instances, all the gains evaporate.

The key assumption of current programs is that ADD/ADHD (IA/HM) children have a disease. Recall that most researchers are abandoning the use of that term and are now using the term "neurobiologically impaired," or "biological disorder," which to the layman means just about the same thing as "disease." If the children are viewed as impaired or sick, the fundamental assumption of current treatments is that they can't function on their own. Therefore, they need medicine and lots of help. To provide this help, current treatments focus on preceding stimuli in the forms of constant coaching, reminding, warning, helping, coaxing, assisting, and cueing.

These prevailing methods began with Russell Barkley around 1980, and almost every approach by every author has varied little from his basic formula. No matter which book you pick up, with careful reading you'll see that they say pretty much the same thing.

In my writings I've used the case of Helen Keller to demonstrate the fundamental problem with this conceptualization. Perhaps you've read the play or seen the movie *The Miracle Worker*. Helen was almost feral, like an animal.

Because of a severe illness as a baby, she lost her sight, hearing, and ability to speak. She was locked in a shell. Unable to control her as she got older, her parents hired a skilled teacher named Annie Sullivan.

Miss Sullivan couldn't work with Helen in the presence of her parents. They saw her as sick and handicapped, and they consequently treated her as an invalid. They constantly helped her, waited on her, and babied her. So Miss Sullivan needed to separate Helen from the pampering of her parents. She saw Helen as normal underneath this impenetrable shell, and if she was going to be of any help, she had to withdraw Helen from her parents and live and work with her in a small cottage away from the main house.

Annie was firm. She stopped pampering Helen. She made Helen function. The result was one of our greatest heroines.

This is considered to be the first documented case of behavior modification.

Let's look at how current behavioral approaches incorporate constant coaching, coaxing, prompting, cueing, reminding, and warning, just the way Helen Keller's parents did. Visual aids are almost always included. For example, Barkley's (1995) parenting techniques include composing chore cards as reminders of household jobs. Barkley's recommendations also include the child's repeating parental commands; reminding the child that he isn't behaving correctly; warning him if discipline is imminent; and reminding and reviewing with the child how he should behave before entering public places.

Harvey Parker's (1994) techniques borrow heavily from Barkley. His approach includes warnings of impending discipline, warning the child that she will get a spanking if she leaves Time Out, and discussing her choices if she does not wish to comply with the parent's command (which later we'll see reinforces oppositional behavior). Parker also recommends using a bathroom for Time Out: I've stated repeatedly in my writings that this is not at all a good idea because in the bathroom are dangerous things, such as pills and razors, and many objects that can be played with and are, therefore, reinforcing rather than punishing the child. Parker also recommends a self-monitoring technique, where the child takes a cassette tape to school that beeps periodically to remind her to pay attention and behave correctly.

Tom Phelan (1984) popularized the "1-2-3 Time Out" method, where one counts or gives three warnings prior to enforcing Time Out.

Hallowell and Ratey (1994) recommend establishing a very structured environment for the ADD/ADHD (IA/HM) child, with abundant use of lists, notes, color-coding objects, and reminder file cards. They also recommend tolerating the child's bad moods, which, we'll learn later, reinforces the child's saying all the wrong kinds of things. Furthermore, they recommend using Time Out only when the parent is upset and cannot handle the child in a calm manner. These techniques only contribute to a confusing and inconsistent environment for the child. We'll later learn that *inconsistency breeds persistency*, which means that these inconsistent techniques strengthen and lock in the very behaviors we're trying to get rid of.

Josephine Wright (1997) advocates that parents ignore temper tantrums and other disruptive behaviors and then discuss the problem with the child once he has calmed down. This actually allows behaviors that shouldn't be occurring to continue. These are inappropriate ways for children to express feelings. Giving attention to or socially reinforcing the temper tantrums or any other disruptive behavior violates basic behavioral principles, because the reinforcement then locks in the inappropriate verbal patterns. Diana Hunter (1995) also recommends discussing children's expressions of feelings, which sounds nice on the surface but winds up reinforcing and increasing inappropriate verbal patterns such as "poor me" statements or negativism. In chapter 7 we'll learn how to talk correctly with children about feelings. Years ago, Greenspoon (1955) demonstrated how we can inadvertently reinforce, shape, or teach children inappropriate verbal patterns.

The vast majority of current methods recommend using a Token Economy program. Barkley and Parker are particular advocates of this approach with ADD/ADHD (IA/HM) children, and it seems every other writer has mimicked the concept. In this approach the child is given some type of symbolic token, such as check marks, happy faces on a chart, or poker chips following a good behavior. The tokens are saved and later used to purchase a toy or an activity that the child likes. Rules are usually posted on a large chart and placed in convenient locations. This may sound nice, but there are unsound methodological errors built in that make matters worse for the ADD/ADHD (IA/HM) child, and we'll look at them shortly. Furthermore, I view token programs as an unnatural and inappropriate model for raising children. During our early years we learn the roles and behaviors for normal family life, and charts and tokens don't present a family environment that is normal. I view families governed by the use of tokens as a rather silly and dysfunctional model of family life. As

Janet Geringer-Woititz (1983) points out, if the child grows up in an inappropriate family environment, then as an adult she won't understand what normal is.

LACK OF RESEARCH ON PARENTING

Here's a real shocker. All the parenting recommendations made by these writers have not been researched. A careful review of the research literature in psychology and psychiatry fails to reveal the existence of any articles specifically focused on the development of truly effective parenting techniques. Hundreds of articles exist that repeat Barkley's basic formula, acknowledging nevertheless that these favored methods don't work and that pills must be added to obtain any results. If any research on truly effective parenting exists, it has not been properly shared with the professional community. Why have techniques proven to not work been repeatedly applied as treatment? Why has the professional community been so hasty to research the effectiveness of drugs with these children, while apparently being in no hurry to develop effective and comprehensive parent management programs? Why has a change in treatment direction not been considered? The CSP is, to date, the only parent training approach designed to work without drugs. It has been properly published in a professional journal and presented at professional conferences. I want the professional community to scrutinize and examine the CSP. It is my fondest wish to encourage other professionals to research and improve these techniques even more.

Is it any wonder that currently popular parenting recommendations don't work well, since they haven't been properly tried, tested, refined, and improved through careful research?

The only research done on currently popular approaches is to plug the techniques into a piece of research designed to highlight how treatment dramatically improves when the drugs are added. Once the ADD/ADHD (IA/HM) children are drugged, they are then more amenable to complying with the coaching, reminding, helping, assisting, and coaxing. Neither the drugs nor the popular behavioral methods are designed to help the child think and function independently. These methods do not help the child to change and to function properly. The combination of drugs and popular behavioral methods only makes the children, as Peter Breggin points out (1998), "compliant robots."

As I have stated, drugs constrain behavior; they teach nothing. While the children are on the drugs, parents are deluded into believing they are better. They are not. When the drugs are stopped, apparent gains collapse. No wonder more and more of the children have to remain on the drugs and programs that provide excessive assistance into adolescence and adulthood.

How These Models Handicap the ADD/ADHD (IA/HM) Child

Claude Steiner (1974) wrote that one of the worst ways we can handicap a child is to make him dependent. This is exactly what these approaches are doing.

The ADD/ADHD (IA/HM) child is unmotivated and unthinking. The approaches cited above only teach the child to comply with the coaxing, prompting, and reminding of the adults. The child learns to rely on all this help. He'll comply with what is being commanded, but he won't learn to remember or be aware of what's going on by himself. He'll comply but become increasingly dependent on assistance. These approaches only heighten his dependency and helplessness. By overhelping him, we handicap him for the rest of his life. Again, is it any wonder we're seeing more and more ADD/ADHD (IA/HM) children who have to stay on drugs as adolescents and adults? They haven't learned to function on their own.

Dependencies

With the emphasis on excessive helping, the ADD/ADHD (IA/HM) child can develop any combination of four types of dependencies.

1. TASK DEPENDENCY involves the child's being unable to initiate or remain focused on specific tasks without someone guiding her throughout the entire process. Doing homework is probably the most problematic task, with class work running a close second. The sequence begins by the child being unable to organize her materials to begin doing the homework (or class work). The parent (or teacher) starts the process by gently showing the child how to place the books, how to put her notepad in front of her, and how to have her pens and pencils neatly placed for easy access. Then the coaching starts. What subject would you like to begin with? What

questions do you need to answer? Where can you find the answers?

On and on it goes, repeating the scene day after day. Usually the child portrays an Academy Award–winning act of a total inability to do anything by herself, and usually the parent buys it. I've seen countless children perform these tasks by themselves once they are required to with the CSP. In initial sessions parents tell me, "He really tries, but he just can't do it by himself. I've seen him sit by his work for hours, crying because he just doesn't understand." I know this is painful for a parent to watch, but a child has to function on his own. You're not going to be there for his entire life. He can learn to do it if required to. The CSP will help make this happen.

Consider this. If a child is blind, should you do everything for him? Or should you teach and require him to perform on his own? Which gives him the best chance for survival?

Why is it that many ADD/ADHD (IA/HM) children begin to perform well near the end of the academic year when they discover that their teacher is considering not promoting them? I've seen numerous improvements miraculously materialize.

Are there lots of tasks that your child likes doing that he performs well without any assistance? Can he set up his video games and follow the complex sequence of skills necessary to win the game? I still can't figure out how to play my boys' games, because the instructions are so complex. Why is your child able to do these things without your help?

In the CSP you'll only act as a resource for

homework when your child asks for assistance. You don't sit with her. She can and will perform well. Soon, when you actually witness these changes, your views about ADD/ADHD (IA/HM) will dramatically change. Maybe at first she'll have to struggle harder, but remember, she must learn to function on her own.

2. COGNITIVE/BEHAVIORAL DEPENDENCY involves the child's failing to remember how to behave correctly without being reminded, throughout the day and throughout changing environments, such as going into a grocery store. Current approaches advocate discussing and reviewing with him how he should behave before entering a new environment: "Now, Billy, we're going into the supermarket. Please tell Mommy how you should behave. What are you going to do with the shopping cart? Are you supposed to touch the cans?" You'll find with the CSP that he can behave well in all circumstances. He can pay attention to his surroundings and to his own behaviors. He can monitor himself. Reminding him is not helping him; it's handicapping him.

3. EMOTIONAL DEPENDENCY involves a child's developing a deeply rooted belief that she must always have someone take care of her. She believes she can't function without a helpmate. The intensity of this belief can range from mild to severe. Current behavioral approaches for ADD/ADHD (IA/HM) often nudge this belief into the more severe end of the continuum. We all have some degree of emotional dependency, but when it reaches the level that we *must* have someone with us throughout life, it can be quite disabling. Being a very dependent per-

son can underlie making rash and desperate choices for partners later in life. Helping a child to become too emotionally dependent is not a good idea.

The rationale for the CSP is not to make a child detached and strong like John Wayne, but to help her feel secure and that she can take care of herself. Part of the CSP philosophy is that one can be sensitive, caring, and loving while at the same time fostering security and self-sufficiency. Al Bandura (1981 and 1986) calls the belief that one is capable of taking care of oneself self-efficacy, and developing a strong sense of it is one of the most important goals of the CSP. Constantly coaching and reminding the ADD/ADHD (IA/HM) child defeats this goal.

4. DEPENDENCY ON MEDICATION is also an important concern. This is not about the drug abuse or addiction issue. This is about developing the *belief that one can't function unless one takes one's pills.* If this false belief is strongly internalized by the ADD/ADHD (IA/HM) child, then it will be difficult for him to abandon taking the pills as he grows older. He will be convinced throughout his life that he must take his pills to perform his job successfully. I've witnessed the evolution of this nonsensical belief in too many children, and frankly, it scares me.

The CSP is an enabling program. It makes the child pay attention, perform well, and be self-reliant without any drugs. Aren't these crucial goals you would like for your child to achieve?

Current Treatments Violate
Correct Behavioral Principles

Something I find very interesting is that current popular behavioral treatments violate basic rules of behavior modification or what is called *social learning theories*. These intrinsic, or built-in, methodological problems explain not only why these approaches don't work but also why they can actually make matters worse.

Recall our discussion about current recommendations to give warnings about misbehaviors, about discussing choices with the child if she doesn't wish to comply with a command, and about discussing her feelings when she becomes upset. Each of these methods requires social interaction with the child at the time of a misbehavior. This interaction provides inadvertent and unintentional social reinforcement that maintains or even increases the misbehaviors. The child is getting attention when misbehaving. Therefore, the misbehaviors are either maintained as a habit or they increase and become more severe.

We learned long ago that interactions with a child at the time of a misbehavior actually reinforces that behavior. Techniques should be designed to minimize interaction and eliminate, as much as possible, every chance of reinforcing inappropriate behaviors. Current approaches reinforce talking back, defiant behaviors, temper tantrums, and inappropriate verbal behaviors. I've asked myself many times: Why are the developers of these techniques making such basic errors? I'll state this frankly: If they were to take my course in behavior modification, they'd be lucky to make a D.

Current approaches advocate ignoring temper tantrums and using Time Out only when a parent feels unable to handle the child's misbehavior and recommending that parents learn to tolerate children's bad moods. Long ago psychologists established principles called *intermittent schedules of reinforcement*, which are designed to strengthen a behavior, preferably a desired behavior, after it has been well learned. In the days of basic behavioral psychology the idea was to deliberately lengthen the periods of time for reinforcing between occurrences of a behavior and to make the child work harder and harder to earn a reinforcement. In addition, the reinforcement timing was deliberately designed to be inconsistent, so the child has to continuously behave correctly while not knowing when the reinforcement is going to occur. This strengthens the behavior, or increases its resistance to being extinguished, that is, being decreased. These techniques are deliberately used when we want to strengthen a proper behavior. *Unfortunately, current techniques have unknowingly been designed to strengthen undesired misbehaviors because of unintentional intermittent reinforcement.* They work in direct opposition to what we should be trying to accomplish. They increasingly lock in and worsen the child's misbehaviors. Such an unfortunate outcome of tenacious misbehaviors leads to the child's being more and more reliant on drugs to subdue the ADD/ADHD (IA/HM) behaviors.

The CSP is carefully designed to avoid this inadvertent mistake, to increase proper behaviors, improve awareness and active thinking, eliminate inappropriate misbehaviors, and increase self-sufficiency without inadvertently reinforcing ADD/ADHD (IA/HM) behaviors.

THE CAREGIVERS' SKILLS PROGRAM

The Caregivers' Skills Program is a carefully designed parenting program planned specifically to control and motivate the ADD/ADHD (IA/HM) child without drugs. It works because everything in it has evolved from over twenty-five years of working with hundreds of these children. All concepts have been refined over and over again; the program has been constantly improved to its current level. It's practical. It's sensible. It's easy to learn and implement. And it is based on sound behavioral principles.

It's called a caregivers' program because it is designed to train all people who take care of the ADD/ADHD (IA/HM) child. It is preferable if all people who are with the child for a significant amount of time each day read the book and follow the program. This then provides consistency and reduces confusion for the child.

Grandparents and older teenagers often care for the children after school. I've had them go through the training along with the parents. I used to do the training with fifteen families at a time, but I've slowed down considerably in the last few years. Ex-spouses have proved to be a challenge; sometimes they willingly go through the training, and sometimes they refuse. If that happens, the CSP still works for the primary custodial parent, although it would be preferable for the other parent to also learn the program.

Many of the weaknesses inherent in currently popular approaches are corrected in the CSP. I don't want the children only to comply. I want them to think, be aware, evaluate, make decisions, and behave themselves. CSP focuses on cognitions as well as on behaviors. I want children, whenever possible, to be off the drugs!

Figure 5.1 shows the outline of our three basic topics: (1) how to clearly target specific behaviors we're going to change; (2) how to develop positive or reinforcing techniques to improve the types of behaviors we want in our children; (3) how to use proper discipline techniques specifically designed to eliminate the high rate of ADD/ADHD (IA/HM) misbehaviors. Additional topics we will cover include teaching children a love for education (called valuing education), developing their love for reading, and teaching them basic values that all children need to learn (called

---

FIGURE 5. 1

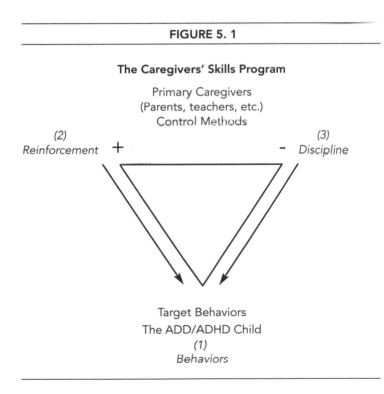

The Caregivers' Skills Program

Primary Caregivers
(Parents, teachers, etc.)
Control Methods

(2)   *(3)*
Reinforcement **+**   **–** *Discipline*

Target Behaviors
The ADD/ADHD Child
(1)
Behaviors

---

value education). Value training is essential to motivate children. If children have firmly learned proper values, they never become ADD/ADHD (IA/HM) in the first place.

An important feature of the CSP is training the children to THINK. The program is designed to activate their brain cells. We're going to teach them to pay attention, evaluate what is going on around them, and self-control their behaviors. Our children can learn to think and function well at home, at school, and everywhere. Consider that their thinking or cognitive abilities are like muscles, and the rule is "Use It or Lose It!" ADD/ADHD (IA/HM) children can be both responsible and accountable for their behaviors. They are not sick. They can pay attention and behave properly. I've witnessed this countless times with the CSP. It's not a magical dream. It's a reality.

Remember that current behavioral approaches don't work unless a child is on drugs, and the drugs never teach children how to think. With the CSP, they'll learn how to think and how to behave responsibly without the use of any drugs.

In the next chapter we're going to identify the specific Target Behaviors we're going to work on.

CHAPTER 6

Targeting the Behaviors of the ADD/ADHD (IA/HM) Child

I N ORDER TO SET GOALS and know that we are succeeding, we have to accomplish two things: first, precisely identify what we're working on; and second, know our procedures and techniques, which we'll cover in chapters 7, 8, and 9. The first component is the Target Behaviors that can be seen and heard.

In this chapter, we'll identify those behaviors engaged in by ADD/ADHD (IA/HM) children that are problematic. We'll look at the patterns of these Target Behaviors, and we'll learn specific goals we want to achieve with each of these behaviors.

Throughout this book I'll highlight where I've made major changes from currently popular approaches. One of these changes involves focusing on a different set of Target Behaviors. Current approaches focus primarily on behaviors that occur most often in school, which are the *DSM-IV* behaviors in Table 4.1, with little emphasis on home behaviors. The CSP reverses this and focuses intensely on home behaviors and getting those under control before focusing on school behaviors. As I explain other major changes I've made, you'll begin to see why the CSP works so well.

At the end of our journey through this book, I hope you'll say, as most of the parents of my ADD/ADHD (IA/HM) children have said, "He's not only well behaved, but he seems so much happier."

TARGET BEHAVIORS

Target Behaviors are habitual, frequent, inappropriate, and clearly observable. They can be seen or heard. Occasional misbehaviors are the trademark of all children but are not generally to be targeted. We're focusing on misbehaviors that occur regularly and frequently in ADD/ADHD (IA/HM) children.

In the CSP program, we're going to make a major shift away from focusing on the behaviors listed in the *DSM-IV*. Refer to Table 4.1. The five basic reasons for the change from the *DSM-IV* behaviors to the CSP behaviors are:

1. The *DSM-IV* behaviors generally occur in school where the parents can't exert control. Teachers have too many students to adequately spend the time and

do the work needed to change the ADD/ADHD (IA/HM) child. Parents have the time and the motivation to work with their own child within the home.

2. It is essential to establish the parents as authorities for the ADD/ADHD (IA/HM) child. By focusing on behaviors in the home, it is the parents who regain the ability to control the child. The CSP program is not punitive, but it is firm and rigorous. The parent is the boss and, as Harry Truman would have said, "That's all there is to it." ADD/ADHD (IA/HM) children want to know the boundaries of their behavior. They want to know right from wrong. They want the security of their parents' being in charge. Some schools of psychology have taken away from parents the responsibility of being in charge. The CSP is giving it back. A structured home with parents in charge helps a child to feel "safe."

3. The behaviors listed in the *DSM-IV* occur too late in the sequence to gain control over the child. A child is too out of control by the time he is pushing, getting out of his seat, and blurting out answers. Then it's too difficult to calm him down and get him back under control. In the CSP, the parent intervenes and establishes control at the mere hint of disruption, not following commands, or being disrespectful. This is a strict approach, but also a very loving one. Knowing his limits not only produces a feeling of security in a child, but because parents in the CSP are deliberately reinforcing the child, he also feels very loved.

Since ADD/ADHD (IA/HM) children are generally obnoxious, they engender the wrath of almost everyone, including peers, teachers, and even parents. By being well behaved and knowing their limits, they are more likable to all those around them. This contributes considerably to their significantly improved self-esteem. Early intervention in the behavioral sequence and the rigor of the CSP are two more major differences compared to other popular programs.

4. Some of the behaviors listed in the *DSM-IV* are poorly defined; they are unclear and too vague for proper behavioral intervention. For example, failing to pay attention is at the core of ADD/ADHD (IA/HM) disorders. But according to proper behavioral techniques, in order to work with children behaviors must be defined more clearly, so that we can observe the behavior. In the CSP paying attention is divided into three specific behaviors:

   a. Visual attention. Are their eyes on their work or on the speaker?
   b. Auditory attention. Can they answer the question "What did you just hear me say?"
   c. Remembering. Being able to answer the question "What should you be doing?"

   Failing any of these easily observable components means the parent will enforce proper consequences.

5. In the CSP program, my research shows that once the ADD/ADHD (IA/HM) children are well controlled at home, then for 80 percent of them schoolwork and school conduct also automatically improve. This is called generalization, meaning that improve-

ments in one environment transfer to other environments. Other writers claim that parenting approaches don't adequately improve school problems or generalize to other environments. This is true; current approaches don't improve school behaviors because the child is never fully brought under control at home in the first place.

In the remaining 20 percent of the children I've worked with, behaviors improve at home but not at school. In other words, the improvements did not generalize. The CSP then adds a Daily Report Card program, where the teachers communicate in a quick and easy way to the parents the child's performance and conduct in school, and the parents carry out meaningful firm consequences at home. This method rarely fails.

THE CSP TARGET BEHAVIORS

There are patterns in the behaviors of ADD/ADHD (IA/HM) children. They cluster together and are grouped into four basic patterns. As we define each of the behaviors and why they're grouped together, you'll begin to see your own ADD/ADHD (IA/HM) child. Families I've trained often ask me if I have an x-ray machine that can see what goes on in their homes. Of course I don't; it's just that these are the most common behavioral characteristics of the ADD/ADHD (IA/HM) child that both the *DSM-IV* and current behavioral approaches neglect to address.

The seventeen specific Target Behaviors, grouped in clusters, are:

GROUP I: ACTIVE MANIPULATIONS
1. Noncompliance—not doing what the parent commands
2. Oppositionalism—defying the parent
3. Temper tantrums

GROUP II: VERBAL MANIPULATIONS
4. "Poor me" statements
5. Negative statements
6. Nagging
7. Interruptions
8. Physical complaints—saying they're ill when they aren't

GROUP III: INATTENTION BEHAVIORS
9. Not paying attention
   a. visual inattention
   b. auditory inattention
   c. failure to remember
10. Helplessness and dependency
11. Poor school performance
12. Poor reading skills

GROUP IV: OTHER COMMON MISBEHAVIORS
13. Dawdling or being late for activities, especially school mornings
14. Tattling
15. Sibling fights
16. Aggression
17. Lying

The number of Target Behaviors will be less for ADD (IA) children than for ADHD (HM) children. ADD (IA) children aren't openly defiant nor are they characterized by the more overt misbehaviors. They mostly tune out and don't pay attention. They are also highly skilled at feigning an inability to organize their work or to understand the material. ADHD (HM) children do these same things and they wreak havoc on their surroundings.

We're going to define and explain each Target Behavior. We'll also discuss relevant issues that will help you understand why these behaviors occur and what can happen if they remain unchecked. We'll also talk about the firm but realistic goals we will establish for each behavior. Our goals are strict because allowing latitude confuses the children about where their boundaries are. We can't get them under control if we're lenient—then nothing will work. Once they are under control, lots of positive things will be coming their way from everyone around them—you, their teachers, their friends, and their relatives. Getting them quickly under control is the kindest thing we can do for them. In addition, they will no longer be viewed as strange, odd, or sick. And most important, they won't need any drugs. If you carry out the CSP correctly, you'll see these changes less than two weeks after starting the program.

Keep these benefits in mind as you enforce the program. It will help motivate you.

A major feature of the CSP is that we target any and all behaviors simultaneously. This is another major difference from current approaches. *Getting them completely under control is essential. Be thorough. Be comprehensive. Allow nothing to slip by.*

Before I discuss each of the behaviors, it's important to understand a very basic concept in behavioral psychology. *Any behavior that occurs consistently or increases over time is being reinforced.* In the chapters that follow, I'll show you the variety of ways that we inadvertently reinforce the Target

Behaviors. If some behaviors like nagging your child wear you down until you give in and he gets what he wants, he is reinforced. Sometimes your child refuses to do as you ask and you end up doing it; therefore, she's "wormed her way" out of doing something she doesn't like, which reinforces her refusal. By not disciplining behaviors correctly, you're inadvertently reinforcing the very behavior you're trying to get rid of, and this is one of the main reasons that currently popular behavioral approaches don't work well.

*Keep this principle in mind as you check each of the boxes for those Target Behaviors that apply to your child.

GROUP I: ACTIVE MANIPULATIONS

In this group of behaviors your child increasingly defies you until he wins by getting his way. Maybe he doesn't win each time, but he's learned over the long run how to get his way or how to get your attention. Place a check mark in the box for each Target Behavior that applies to your child.

1. □ NONCOMPLIANCE — NOT DOING WHAT YOU COMMAND

   ADD (IA): common; ADHD (HM): very common

   With the ADD/ADHD (IA/HM) child do you find yourself repeating commands until you wind up screaming? Does the following seem familiar?

   > "Johnny, please pick up your toys, it's time for dinner." No response. Two minutes pass by.
   > In a more irritated tone, "Johnny, I said pick up the toys, dinner is ready." No response. Two minutes pass by.

Loudly, "Johnny pick up the blasted toys and get to the table." No response. Two minutes pass by.

Screaming, "If those damn toys are not picked up this instant, I'm going to whale the daylights out of you!"

Finally he complies, and you end up eating dinner with stomach acid reflux.

Johnny has learned either to tune you out or to ignore you. Much of the time you probably walk over and throw the toys in the toy box, and he wins. Your repeated coaxing gives him lots of your time and attention. He's actually getting reinforced.

Our goal in the CSP is one command given in a normal but firm tone, at which point he *immediately* does as he's been told. I know what you're thinking: "Yeah, right! With an ADD/ADHD (IA/HM) kid, no way!" In fact, you're going to learn how to achieve this strict goal, and with ADD/ADHD (IA/HM) children, it is essential that you do get them to comply immediately. You're the boss. No fussing or fighting will be tolerated. With ADD/ADHD (IA/HM) children, you must be very firm. However, as you'll see in chapter 7, when they immediately comply, they will earn your positive attention. You'll be deliberately reinforcing proper behaviors. The CSP is both firm and positive.

GOAL: One command—immediate compliance.

2. ☐ OPPOSITIONALISM — OPEN DEFIANCE
   ADD (IA): rare; ADHD (HM): very common

Does your child talk back to you? Does he say, "No, I won't. You can't make me!" Does he look you straight in the eye and throw his toy on the floor? This is oppositionalism. Do you find yourself screaming at him whenever he does this? Does your blood boil to the point that you spank him? Does he then cry and finally do as you commanded? And does he do this again the very next day? In chapter 8, we'll discuss punishment, and you'll learn that even though your interactions are negative when you give him your time and attention, you're actually reinforcing him. Ask yourself, "Why is this behavior continuing over and over again?" Remember, if it is recurring, it's getting reinforced.

Our goal with the ADD/ADHD (IA/HM) child is to be very strict. No defiance is permitted. Zero. However, if the child speaks in a positive, assertive fashion, "Dad, can I finish watching my show?" be fair and listen. But if your answer is still no, don't tolerate any defiance.

Notice how oppositionalism involves more active manipulation than noncompliance for your child to win out over you.

GOAL: One command—no defiance.

3. ☐ TEMPER TANTRUMS
ADD (IA): rare; ADHD (HM): very common

Temper tantrums range in severity. They can range from foot stomping, crying, and slamming a door to falling on the floor screaming, to running around the room screaming and breaking things. Temper tantrums are very common in ADHD (HM) children. Attempts at controlling or restraining the child only give her attention and reinforce the behavior. Don't worry; you'll learn how to handle this correctly.

Temper tantrums are highly inappropriate forms of

expressing feelings. They can become a habit and continue into adulthood. Did you know they're the number-one cause of divorce?

Asserting himself is the correct way for a child to express a feeling. "Mommy, I'm mad at you because you're not listening to me," is reasonable. Temper tantrums are not.

We can expect no more than five temper tantrums per year, and even then they should be associated with a child's being overstressed or out of sorts because she may be becoming ill. Moms are better at detecting this than dads. Many ADHD (HM) children have several temper tantrums each week. Even one per month is too many. In the CSP we are going to be strict indeed. This behavior is intolerable and needs to be stopped, but drugging children with amphetamines is not the way to stop it. We'll learn more intelligent ways to stop temper tantrums.

Again, notice how ADD/ADHD (IA/HM) children have actively escalated their manipulating.

GOAL: No more than five temper tantrums in a year.

GROUP II: VERBAL MANIPULATIONS

This group of Target Behaviors involves a variety of verbal gymnastics so the child can either get his way or get your attention. This is an alternative pattern highly favored by ADD/ADHD (IA/HM) children when the more brutish active manipulations aren't working well for them.

4. ☐ "POOR ME" STATEMENTS

ADD (IA): very common; ADHD (HM): very common

These statements are designed to make you feel sorry for your child, to win your sympathy and to get her way. Whenever I hear a parent tell me during an initial session, "He's such a sensitive child," I know we're dealing with an expert at "poor me" verbal patterns. Think about whether you occasionally give in to these kinds of statements; they can be hard to resist:

"You don't love me."
"You hate me."
"No one loves me."
"I can't do anything right."
"Why am I always wrong?"
"Why do you love my brother more than me?"
"Daddy hates me."
"No one at school likes me."
"I'm dumb."
"Everyone hates me."
"I want to die."
"I'm going to kill myself."

Do these sound familiar? If the last two statements occur, it's best to consult a professional who can assess whether there is a risk of danger or if they are merely stronger "poor me" statements designed to get the child's way.

Also included as "poor me's" are: pouting, whining, and manipulative crying, where the child is easily wounded and moved to tears. Crying because of falling down or some other physical injury doesn't count.

When "poor me" statements occur only rarely, do not consider them a Target Behavior. Children can become tired, overstressed, or ill, and at those times they need comforting. However, when "poor me's" are frequent and manipulative, we cannot allow them to continue. If they are habitual the child will eventually begin to believe how terrible she is and how bad her life is; this is called *internalizing*, and it can occur by age ten. Once internalized, these statements turn into beliefs, and then they often result in a depressed teenager or adult.

By repeatedly making these statements, a child loses the capacity to distinguish between manipulation and true feelings. Eventually, if allowed to continue, she won't feel well much of the time. She'll feel sad, down, or depressed.

We're often told that depression is a disease. Can you see, however, that through verbal rehearsal a child can learn to see himself and the world in a depressed way? He develops an underlying pattern of depressed thoughts or cognitions. When that happens, treatment becomes difficult. This is one way that low self-esteem develops in the ADD/ADHD (IA/HM) child.

To reestablish a child's ability to distinguish real feelings from manipulations, this form of verbal rehearsal must be completely stopped for about four months before allowing an occasional expression of feelings.

GOAL: "Poor me" statements only once or twice a month, but only after not permitting any for an initial period of four months.

5. □ Negative Statements

ADD (IA): common; ADHD (HM): very common

While "poor me" statements are directed inward, about the child himself, negative statements are directed outward, toward other people. These statements include some of the following:

"I hate you."

"I hate my brother."

"Why do we always have to go to the mall?"

"She's stupid."

"I hate doing this."

"You're mean."

"School's boring."

Once again, an occasional negative statement is not a Target Behavior. Only when you hear it several times a week is it a habit or pattern that requires correction. If allowed to continue, then it can also become internalized as part of your child's beliefs. And then you will most likely see a child who is angry, hostile, critical, bitter, and cynical. Once these characteristics are locked in, it becomes increasingly difficult to reverse them.

Think about how few adults or children would want to be around such a negative person. By allowing negative verbalizations to continue, you're most likely condemning your child to being disliked and shunned by others. It's a good idea to correct these statements now. They only add to the ADD/ADHD (IA/HM) child not being liked by others.

GOAL: Only rare expressions of about two per month, but then only after an initial period of four months where none are allowed.

6. ☐ NAGGING

ADD (IA): common; ADHD (HM): very common

I'll bet that you can already see how nagging gets reinforced. By pressuring you, your child knows you'll eventually wear down and give in. This is one of the more obnoxious patterns of the ADD/ADHD (IA/HM) child.

Whenever you tell your child "no," it is important to give him a good reason. If you can't think of a reason, reconsider your answer. You have power over your child, and it can be very frustrating for him if you often say "no" without helping him understand why. Be fair. Be sensible. But if you've said "no" with a good reason, then that's the end of the discussion.

GOAL: No nagging permitted.

7. ☐ INTERRUPTING

ADD (IA): rare; ADHD (HM): very common

Interrupting can be one of the most annoying behaviors in the repertoire of the ADD/ADHD (IA/HM) child. Picking up the extension phone and butting in while you are talking to someone else isn't very pleasant. Saying, "Mommy, Mommy, Mommy" while you're talking to someone is very annoying and very impolite. Interrupting should only be permitted if something dangerous is occurring or if there's an emergency.

GOAL: No interruptions.

8. ☐ PHYSICAL COMPLAINTS

ADD (IA): fairly common; ADHD (HM): fairly common

Complaining about not feeling well when it's really not true can be an easily reinforced verbal behavior. The

ADD (IA) or ADHD (HM) child hates school, and being sick is the best way to get out of going. As with any verbal pattern, if it is allowed to continue, it can become internalized, and you could wind up with a full-blown hypochondriac on your hands.

Make certain that your child isn't truly ill. If she isn't, send her to school and treat this verbal pattern, if frequent, as a Target Behavior.

GOAL: No physical complaints unless they are valid.

GROUP III: INATTENTION BEHAVIORS

Not paying attention and not thinking are at the core of ADD/ADHD (IA/HM) problems. It means the child's mind is not focused on his work or his surroundings. His attention is elsewhere, like daydreaming. Not thinking means he has not thought about what behaviors he is doing, the consequences of those behaviors, and their impact on others. Imposing consequences on all Target Behaviors requires the ADD/ADHD (IA/HM) child to attend to his behaviors and to remember the consequences for misbehaving. If he fails to actively remain aware of his behaviors and forgets impending consequences, then they will keep occurring until he finally begins to remember and control himself. Once this self-attending and awareness is activated, his overall functioning improves dramatically and remains improved without any need for stimulant drugs.

In this grouping we'll be focusing on inattention both at home and at school.

9. ☐ Not Paying Attention

ADD (IA): very common; ADHD (HM): very common

In order to work on this Target Behavior we need to dissect inattention into the three more concrete behaviors below:

a. ☐ *Visual inattention, or not looking*

The child's eyes must be on her schoolwork or on the speaker. At home that is the parent, and at school the teacher. At home this applies to homework; at school to class work. It will be necessary to work on this and the other two attentional behaviors at school only if your child is not among the 80 percent whose schoolwork automatically improves within four weeks after the CSP has been started at home.

Goal: A strict requirement that her eyes be on her task or the speaker, with only very brief diversions.

b. ☐ *Auditory inattention, or not listening*

The ADD/ADHD (IA/HM) child can look you straight in the eye and not hear a thing that you say. To check if he's tuned you out, simply ask, "What did I just say?"

Goal: He must be able to repeat what was just said.

c. ☐ *Not Remembering*

There are two types of memory skills that are imperative for the ADD/ADHD (IA/HM) child to master. The first is *Task Memory*, which requires memorizing academic materials. The second is *Cognitive/ Behavioral Memory*, where the child must remember how to behave correctly in all social settings.

119

Task Memory

Can the ADD (IA) or ADHD (HM) child memorize? Yes! Yes! Yes! It takes deep concentration and lots of energy to memorize her schoolwork. She does not have a disease or a neurobiological disorder that prevents this. ADD/ADHD (IA/HM) children can sometimes put on Academy Award–winning performances feigning an inability to memorize and concentrate, but don't buy their act.

I've met many ADD (IA) adults who are convinced that they need their pills to help them concentrate and memorize, but they can do this without pills. These are skills that can be learned and mastered with diligent practice. Memorizing and concentrating are crucial skills for almost all academic work, and the optimal time for learning them is as a child. For the child who hasn't learned them, it will require more effort on his part to master them. If we convince a child he has a disease and can't do it, he may give up ever really trying.

I've heard from countless parents that they watch their ADD/ADHD (IA/HM) child struggle with his schoolwork but that he just can't seem to retain the material. In the absence of a low IQ or damage to the eyes or ears, your child can indeed learn deep concentration and memorization skills. But when you sit with him and coach, cajole, plead, assist, prompt, and overly assist he will never learn how to concentrate and memorize. These are skills that must be mastered. It is not magic. If your child has trouble concentrating and memorizing, then he may have to work extremely hard until he does master these skills. Then he'll be able to use these abilities for the rest of his life. Once the skill is mastered, it becomes easier. At first it may take considerable effort.

Actually, ADD/ADHD (IA/HM) children already know how to concentrate and memorize. They readily memorize the complex steps for video games, board games, and other activities they like and enjoy. But they don't memorize schoolwork because they hate it. They will fight you to the bitter end to convince you that they just can't do their schoolwork. I've seen countless cases where we implemented the school program for these children, and with the proper consequences of the CSP they indeed demonstrated that they could concentrate and memorize.

Cognitive/Behavioral Memory

Remembering also applies to all Target Behaviors, because the ADD/ADHD (IA/HM) child should remember how to correctly behave at all times in all locations. With the right consequences, he'll learn to how to behave correctly everywhere and anywhere in less than two weeks after parents begin implementing the CSP.

GOAL: To concentrate on and memorize their schoolwork whenever required, and to remember to behave correctly at all times.

10. ☐ HELPLESSNESS AND DEPENDENCY
    ADD (IA): very common; ADHD (HM): very common

We discussed the issues of helplessness and dependency in the preceding chapter. We talked about four kinds of dependencies: Task Dependency, Cognitive/Behavioral Dependency, Medication Dependency, and Emotional

Dependency. Dependency and helplessness are related to the previous topic of remembering.

If the ADD/ADHD (IA/HM) child learns the requisite concentration and memory skills for her school tasks, then Task Dependency disappears. If she learns how to correctly behave at all times, that is, develops Cognitive/Behavioral Memory without being reminded or coached, then Cognitive/Behavioral Dependency disappears. If she masters these two skills without medication, then Medication Dependency disappears. If she learns to do all these things on her own and with minimal help, then your child develops an enhanced sense of self-confidence and self-reliance that greatly reduces excessive Emotional Dependency.

However, if parents practice the methods of parenting recommended in most currently popular approaches, then all four dependencies escalate and can permanently handicap the ADD/ADHD (IA/HM) child. He must learn to function independently, on his own. Drugs and current approaches are not designed to foster this; they are only making matters worse. Remember what Claude Steiner said: Making a child dependent and helpless is the worst thing we can do to him.

GOAL: No Task Dependency, no Cognitive/Behavioral Dependency, no Medication Dependency, little Emotional Dependency.

Joyce

One of my students, Joyce, came to the front to speak with me immediately after the first class period in the semester.

I'd given out and reviewed the requirements for my Introduction to Psychology course, one of which is called the typing requirement. Long ago I discovered that many of my students were doing poorly on exams because the notes they took were either sparse or extremely inaccurate. Thus, I began requiring that my students carefully and comprehensively outline and type their lecture notes, which I then grade. The accuracy of their notes improved, and so did the average grades in all my classes. I believe this requirement forces students to develop active listening and deep concentration skills. Oddly, the students liked this requirement because it seemed to benefit them in all their other courses as well as in mine.

Joyce said, "Dr. Stein, I have attention deficit disorder; would you allow me to tape-record the lectures to help with this typing requirement?" I gently replied: "No. This is your chance to overcome your mythical ADD. I will help you. Type your notes and bring them to me each week, and I'll help you improve them. I'll also ask one of the students in the class who has done well in my other courses to help you. I want you to overcome this problem. It will take some hard work and dedicated effort at first." By the third week of the semester, she was presenting me with excellent out-lines. She reported feeling proud that she finally learned she could actively listen and concentrate. She also under-stood that she never did have ADD (IA). She got an A in the course and graduated with a 3.2 (about a B) grade-point average.

I have repeated this scenario countless times with students who believed they had an ADD/ADHD (IA/HM) disease and, therefore, would always be handicapped.

11. ☐ POOR SCHOOL PERFORMANCE
ADD (IA): very common; ADHD (HM): very common

Poor school performance is the primary concern parents have with ADD/ADHD (IA/HM) children, and it's usually why they are put on medication. The ADD (IA) child typically makes poor grades, and the ADHD (HM) child makes poor grades and tears up the classroom.

When brought under control at home with the CSP, about 80 percent of the children also immediately show dramatic improvement in their schoolwork and in their school conduct. For them, intervention in the school setting isn't then necessary. However, for the remaining 20 percent, a formal school program will be needed, and it is fully covered in chapter 10.

ADD/ADHD (IA/HM) is basically an attitude and motivation problem. ADD/ADHD (IA/HM) children hate schoolwork, and they have no desire to behave themselves in the school setting. Notice that I didn't say they hate school. Many ADD/ADHD (IA/HM) children like going to school—they just hate doing the work.

GOAL: Passing grades in *all* subjects and no conduct problems. Please note that many of the ADD/ADHD (IA/HM) children I have treated have made As and Bs; we'll discuss how to make that happen for your child.

12. ☐ POOR READING SKILLS
ADD (IA): very common; ADHD (HM): very common

Almost all ADD/ADHD (IA/HM) children hate schoolwork, and many of them also hate reading. Good reading skills are fundamental to education. In chapter 10, I'll offer ten helpful hints for making reading fun and improving their reading skills.

GOAL: To see your child awake after bedtime reading under his blanket with a flashlight.

GROUP IV: OTHER COMMON MISBEHAVIORS

Remember that it is essential that you get all misbehaviors under control in dealing with the ADD/ADHD (IA/HM) child. Any loopholes and the CSP will not work well. The behaviors in this grouping don't lend themselves to a nice, neat package, and I'll just call them Other. However, each Target Behavior in this group is equally as important as every misbehavior we have covered thus far.

13. ☐ DAWDLING

ADD (IA): common; ADHD (HM): common

Is your child late for school almost every morning? Does he take forever to complete his homework? But if you're going to the video arcade, is he usually outside at the car in a flash, waiting for you? Can he put certain games and toys together practically blindfolded, in less than a minute? Again, if there is something he doesn't like doing, he'll take forever to do it. If there is something he loves doing, he'll do whatever is necessary to be ready "faster than a speeding bullet." If you answer "yes" to these questions, do you wonder if ADD/ADHD (IA/HM) is some type of mysterious and highly selective disease?

Dawdling can be controlled without your being

125

constantly aggravated with your child, and later we'll learn how it's done.

GOAL: Only very rare instances of dawdling, and never on school mornings.

14. ☐ TATTLING

ADD (IA): fairly rare; ADHD (HM): fairly common

Tattling is a fairly rare behavior for ADD (IA) children, because they are usually quiet and reserved and don't engender negative reactions from other children. The ADHD (HM) children are usually obnoxious and frequently become the target of wrath from other children. ADHD (HM) children often have poor social skills. Teaching and requiring them to behave in socially correct ways is important to helping them get along better with others. If you respond to their tattling by straightening out their social problems, you're preventing them from learning how to manage their social difficulties and entanglements.

In most instances your best response is to say, "Go handle it yourself." You may want to teach some specific social and verbal skills to your ADD/ADHD (IA/HM) child, but never teach these at the time of tattling or you'll reinforce the tattling. Teach them at a quiet time when your child is well behaved. If you constantly intervene in his social problems, you'll prevent him from becoming involved in the trial and error process of learning appropriate behaviors. Hints for teaching social skills to your child are in chapter 12. If you need more in-depth help, read psychologist Philip Zimbardo's books on shyness.

The only time you should intervene when your child tattles is when something dangerous is involved, such as, "Billy has a bottle of pills," or if aggression is happening.

GOAL: To let him solve his social dilemmas on his own.

15. ☐ SIBLING FIGHTS
ADD (IA): fairly common; ADHD (HM): very common

If there is one universal Target Behavior, sibling fights is it. Trying to completely control the tiffs among siblings would only be an exercise in futility. You can, however, reduce the level of intensity, and you can, and should, fully control any physical aggression.

Don't intervene unless the level of intensity is disruptive and interfering with whatever you're doing. If you're watching TV and you can't hear, it's time to deal with the situation. If you hear, "Keep it down or we'll get in trouble with Mom," then stay out of it.

When intervening, never ask, "What's going on here?" You will only find yourself in the position of the judge in *The People's Court*. By the time both children tell their points of view, you will be thoroughly confused. The best rule is that if you have to intervene, then *both children are disciplined with no questions asked*. One of them instigated, the other reacted, and both are probably "guilty as charged." However, if you actually observed who was the primary culprit, then discipline only that one.

If they have separate rooms, it is helpful to have a standard rule that the children not enter each other's room without permission. They may avoid getting into trouble by withdrawing to their room to remove themselves from an escalating tiff.

Goal: To keep the intensity of sibling fights to mild levels.

16. ☐ Aggression

ADD (IA): rare; ADHD (HM): occasional

In the *DSM-IV*, there is a separate diagnosis for ADD/ADHD (IA/HM) with aggression. This involves arguments with other children that end in a violent altercation. It may involve hitting or throwing an object at someone, so this Target Behavior can become highly dangerous. Aggression should never be permitted unless it's in self-defense.

Because this behavior is usually infrequent, it sometimes doesn't respond solely to the CSP. Therefore, in chapter 11 we'll discuss additional potent steps to get this problem under control.

Goal: No aggression unless in self-defense.

17. ☐ Lying

ADD (IA): fairly common; ADHD (HM): fairly common

The two greatest lies of the ADD/ADHD (IA/HM) child are, "No, Mom, the teacher didn't give us any homework," and "Teacher, I lost my homework on the bus." Does this sound familiar? Most lies involve schoolwork. Lying is usually done to avoid discipline for a misdeed or to obtain something a child wants. Because a child can become more skillful in the art of lying as he gets older, it is best to firmly get this behavior under control as early as possible, while you can more easily tell when he is lying.

Imaginary play and fantasy are normal and should not be targeted.

GOAL: No lying.

REVIEWING YOUR
ADD/ADHD (IA/HM) CHILD'S
TARGET BEHAVIORS

Carefully review all the Target Behaviors you checked. Remember, these are the behaviors that are frequent and habitual. If you are uncertain whether to target a specific behavior, then it is best that you do target it. Thoroughness and comprehensiveness are among the most important reasons why the CSP works while other programs aren't as effective.

ASSESS THE TARGET BEHAVIORS

School performance and conduct will not improve unless almost all Target Behaviors are 90 to 100 percent under control. Generalization will not take place, and it will be useless to start the Daily Report Card program until this level of improvement is reached at home.

The following exercise is crucial and should be conducted separately by each caregiver. First, list all Target Behaviors. Second, each caregiver estimates the percentage of improvement for *each* behavior, with 0 percent being absolutely no improvement, and 100 percent being perfect improvement, with no evidence of the Target Behavior in the last two weeks. Doing this exercise is of utmost importance. Try to be as honest and accurate as you can.

EXAMPLE 1 demonstrates a profile where school performance, conduct, test grades, and homework grades will NOT improve.

TARGET BEHAVIORS	ESTIMATES OF IMPROVEMENT
Noncompliance	70%
Oppositionalism	75%
Temper Tantrums	100%
Poor Me's	85%
Negativisms	85%
Nagging	80%
Interruptions	80%
Physical Complaints	85%
Visual Inattention	70%
Auditory Inattention	65%
Not Remembering	85%
Helplessness	90%
Dawdling	0%
Tattling	80%

Assessing Reading, Sibling Fights, Aggression, and Lying are exceptions. It isn't necessary that they reach the 90 percent mark in order for school behaviors to improve.

EXAMPLE 2 demonstrates when improvement of behaviors at home will most likely generalize to school, or when the Daily Report Card program will work. Neither will occur unless these levels of improvement are reached.

Target Behaviors	Estimates of Improvement
Noncompliance	95%
Oppositionalism	100%
Temper Tantrums	100%
Poor Me's	100%
Negativisms	95%
Nagging	100%
Interruptions	95%
Physical Complaints	90%
Visual Inattention	95%
Auditory Inattention	95%
Not Remembering	90%
Helplessness	90%
Dawdling	100%
Tattling	100%

If your child were a patient in my private practice, I would actually conduct this assessment once a week with you. Only when these high levels of improvement are reached will school behaviors also improve. Don't start the Daily Report Card program until these levels are reached, or you will not get results.

Some people may criticize the CSP as being repressive. It is not at all repressive; in fact, it is an enhancing program. Yes, it's strict, rigorous, and firm, but it will enhance your child's life. First, you won't have to put those awful chemicals into his body. Second, you'll be increasing all of your child's proper behaviors and skills. Third, he will be more likable and, therefore, will evoke more positive reactions from adults and other children. Fourth, he will improve his self-worth and self-image by becoming more self-sufficient and independent. Fifth, his academic work will improve, which adds to his self-esteem. Sixth, all the yelling, threats, and spankings will stop, and the tension in the home will be considerably reduced. And, finally, you will feel more secure in your parenting skills, and tension and stress will be reduced for you and your child.

ADD/ADHD (IA/HM) children want and need proper structure. They benefit when they clearly know right from wrong. Remember to listen carefully to yourself when you say, "She seems so much happier."

In the next chapter we'll learn the principles for improving desired and appropriate patterns of behavior.

CHAPTER 7

Reinforcing
Desired Behaviors

IN THIS CHAPTER we will learn how to interact with ADD/ ADHD (IA/HM) children to increase desirable behaviors. At the end of the last chapter, I mentioned how much happier these children can be. The reason for this is that the CSP relies on natural social reinforcement instead of the mechanical approaches of other programs. The model of the CSP is realistic because it emphasizes normal and healthy parent-child interactions.

Most other programs rely on Token Economy programs, where rules are posted and symbolic rewards or tokens, such as stars, poker chips, or check marks are given for proper behavior. After being accumulated or saved, the tokens are traded in for material reinforcers such as treats, toys, or privileges. Recall our earlier discussion about how the presence of posted rules and symbolic tokens is coun-terproductive, because they serve as constant reminders and cues. This is exactly what we don't want for the ADD/ADHD (IA/HM) child. The Token Economy fosters Task and Cognitive/Behavioral Dependencies. It also empha-sizes material rewards, which I view as paying a child for behaviors he or she should be doing in the normal course of everyday interactions at home and school. In addition, I do not view Token Economy programs as an appropriate model for raising children. They are contrived and artifi-cial, and they do not lay the foundation for a child to learn normal behaviors and interactions of family life.

The only time we'll use material reinforcers is in con-trolling the more tenacious behaviors of aggression and lying *after* the CSP has gotten all other Target Behaviors under control.

WHY CAN'T WE LEARN HOW TO DISCIPLINE NOW?

Be patient about learning discipline. I learned long ago that if I taught discipline to parents too early, they skipped over the most important topic necessary for permanently changing the ADD/ADHD (IA/HM) child, which is social reinforcement. Discipline will only temporarily suppress an inappropriate behavior—reinforcement is the key for teaching a child proper behaviors and motivating him or her to continue them. Soon enough you'll learn potent, strict discipline skills, but this chapter contains the key for real success.

WHAT ARE REINFORCERS?

Reinforcers are rewards that maintain or increase behaviors. Remember what I said earlier about the converse of this rule: Any behavior that is maintained or increasing is being reinforced in some way.

Here is another major change in the CSP versus other popular approaches. If we apply what we just learned about reinforcement, then it becomes clear that by interacting with your child when he is misbehaving you are reinforcing the Target Behaviors you are trying to get rid of. When you discuss his feelings with your child at the moment he makes a "Poor Me" statement, you are maintaining or increasing that verbal pattern. Ask yourself why he constantly repeats all these misbehaviors. The mere act of warning him while misbehavior is occurring gives your child attention for that Target Behavior.

This same rule applies to dependencies. If you sit with your child while she does homework, you are reinforcing Task Dependency. In addition, I'm sure your child keeps saying, "I can't do this," or "This is too hard," or "The teacher didn't teach us this," or she starts crying. Look at all the "Poor Me's" and "negative" statements you are reinforcing. Matters get worse, because she becomes so skillful at making such statements that she has you and herself believing she is misbegotten and unfortunate.

Most currently popular programs are so fraught with errors in proper social learning and behavioral theory that it's hard to believe that psychologists designed them.

Types of Reinforcers

There are two broad categories of reinforcers—social and material. In turn, material reinforcers are divided into activities and objects.

Social	Material	
	Activities	Objects
paying attention	watching TV	toys
spending time with	free play	sweets
a child	going outside	favorite foods
looking at_____	bike riding	a new bike
talking to_____	playing games	tokens (check
touching, such	playing ball	marks, stars,
as hugs and kisses	special privileges,	poker chips)
listening	such as going	
praising	to a movie	
just showing a reaction		

Why Social Reinforcement Is More Important than Material

1. BONDING: Socially reinforcing and praising your child fosters a close and loving relationship. Material reinforcers do not.
2. SUSTAINED IMPROVEMENTS: Material programs don't obtain lasting improvements. Early gains fade quickly because children tire of material reinforcers. This is called the *satiation effect*, and when it happens the child's motivation to behave also wanes. With

social reinforcement, there is no satiation problem, and you can do it anytime and anywhere.

3. PAYMENT EXPECTANCY: A major problem with material programs is the payment expectancy, which is the child's refusal to behave properly unless rewarded. This is a poor value to teach a child. Proper behavior at home and at school should not become something for which a child should expect payment. Children should develop a natural sense of care and concern for others, and they should learn that proper behavior represents respect for those around them. With social reinforcement, there is no payment expectancy. Love, affection, and attention are natural, healthy consequences for behavior. Material reinforcers are artificial contrivances.

4. POSITIVE SELF-IMAGE: ADD/ADHD (IA/HM) children generally have low opinions of themselves. Adults and other children don't like them. Therefore, they need to hear lots of praise and receive lots of hugs. This is exactly what social reinforcement does and what material reinforcement does not do.

PRINCIPLES FOR CORRECTLY REINFORCING

1. IMMEDIACY: Children make mental connections or associations between behaviors and consequences. Therefore, it is best to reinforce while or immediately after a correct behavior occurs. This helps children learn the association and reduces confusion. If you delay praising, then they will associate the praise with the behavior that is going on at

that time and not with the Target Behavior you want to improve. If your son has a Target Behavior of making weird noises at the dinner table, and for the moment he's sitting quietly, don't delay. Say, "Billy, you're sitting so quietly, I'm proud of you." Catch the correct behavior immediately.

2. CONSISTENCY: In the early stages of working with your ADD/ADHD (IA/HM) child, it is extremely important that you consistently and abundantly socially reinforce him. If you fail to work hard at consistently reinforcing correct behaviors, you will not see any improvements. You must work at the CSP, because there are no miracles.

If you're in the grocery store and this is Billy's favorite place to wreak havoc, then constantly reinforce him while at the store. If he's being quiet, tell him, "Billy, you're being so quiet in the store, keep it up." When you're in the canned goods aisle, add, "Billy, you remembered not to touch the cans. You're really trying to be well behaved, aren't you?" While he's walking beside the cart say, "You're not running all over the store. I'm glad you're staying next to me." You will see dramatic changes in your ADD/ADHD (IA/HM) child within two weeks after starting this training. But you'll obtain these results only if you remain highly consistent. If you're not seeing such results, check to see if you're being consistent. Later, as new behaviors become new habits, you can relax a bit about being so extremely consistent. But for the first several weeks, you must keep it up. If you let up too quickly, your child will let you know by starting to misbehave again.

Consistency also means among caregivers. Each caregiver must work at consistently reinforcing. Failing to do so creates an inconsistent and confusing environment for your child, so all caregivers must coordinate and work together.

It is also important to be consistent in different settings: the grocery store, a mall, the car, someone's house. You don't want your child to be well behaved only at home. Reinforce anywhere and everywhere.

3. USING POSITIVE DESCRIPTIVE STATEMENTS: When reinforcing your child, describe in very precise language what he is doing correctly. For example:

> "Billy, I like the way you're sitting at the dinner table. You're being quiet and you're politely asking for things." "I like the way you're behaving in the store. You're staying next to me and you're not touching anything. I'm very proud of you." "Your homework is well done. Your handwriting is neat and you answered all the questions by yourself."

Unfortunately, parents of ADD/ADHD (IA/HM) children are always using descriptive statements, but in the wrong way and at the wrong times. Usually they involve negative statements for improper Target Behaviors, such as:

> "Billy, look at those toys! You scattered them all over the floor. Do you see that toy box? Why can't you pick up some of your toys and put them in the box? Why do I have to always remind you?"

"Chris, will you stop chattering so much? You haven't stopped talking since we got home. All you do is talk, talk, talk. Can't you keep your lips pressed together?"

You may be used to descriptive statements, but unfortunately the negative kind. Now you've got to reverse this and use positive descriptive statements when your child is behaving correctly. This is good for his self-esteem and to improve desired behaviors.

4. TALKING IN A NORMAL MANNER: When socially reinforcing your child, by all means show your pleasure, but don't exaggerate. Stick to your normal style of speaking. Some programs recommend exaggerating your pleasure and speaking in an excessively animated manner. Doing this models inappropriate social-verbal behavior. Younger children are somewhat prone to mimicking this verbal behavior, and such imitation can cause them considerable trouble with other children, one of the last things an ADD/ADHD child needs. Be clear. Be warm. Be natural. Talking in a normal tone also creates a more sedate and calm environment, which is essential for ADD/ADHD (IA/HM) children.

REINFORCING TO HELP YOUR CHILD BE MORE INDEPENDENT

Do you do *everything* for your child? Do you cook for him? do his laundry? clean his room? make his bed? You're missing some wonderful opportunities for teaching many important skills. Believe it or not, you'd be surprised how many complex skills you can teach even an attention deficit hyperactive child. In fact, it is important that you teach them because they help the child feel more self-confident and independent.

It is easier for you to do these chores yourself. Chasing after your child in order to get him to pick up a towel wears you out. I know that. But once you've completed the program described in this book and have gotten him functioning well, you'll be in a position to teach him these skills and require that he perform all of them as a normal part of his sharing in household responsibilities. In the long run, life becomes much easier for you.

Teaching your child a variety of complex self-help and family household skills will have many benefits for her. Performing these skills gives her a sense of accomplishment and enhances her self-esteem. It helps her to function in an independent manner, and it gives her a sense of importance by sharing family responsibilities. Most important, it builds a sense of responsibility, community, and family.

How is the magic done? It's accomplished by using a reinforcing technique called *shaping*. You merely break a complex skill into learnable small steps and reinforce your child for each step learned. Let's look at an example. How do children learn to swim? One way is by the John Wayne School of Aquatics—you throw them into the water and they either swim or drown. Then there is the more sensible way:

1. Sit in the shallow end of the pool.
2. Put your child's face in the water.
3. Have him hold his breath and keep his face in for longer and longer periods.

4. Put his entire head under the water.
5. Stretch his legs out while holding him from beneath.
6. Stretch his arms forward, keeping his face in the water.
7. Do the "dead man's float."
8. Once he can do the float, adding the kicks and arm movements is easy.

The most important part is to praise (reinforce) the child for each improved step. Have you combined this shaping technique with praising for doing housework or schoolwork?

Look at Figure 7.1, a diagram of how shaping works: Small steps for small improvements; praise for improvement at each step. Let's apply it to teaching six-year-old Christine to make her bed.

Step 1 is to find her base level, what she can do without instruction. She doesn't do a very good job. For a six-year-old, this is a complex skill, and it's not likely she can learn the entire process in one session. For Step 2, teach her to perform correctly with the bottom ends of the cover. Have her practice until she masters the step. Reinforce her for her new learned skill. "Christine, the corners look so nice and neat. You did a very good job." Step 3 is pulling the covers evenly across the bed. "Christine, the cover looks so neat and even. Wonderful!" Again, reinforce. You may want to do each step on a separate day. Step 4 is folding the top end of the cover and putting the pillows on top. Reinforce. Step 5 is pulling the cover neatly over the pillows. "Christine, now you can make a bed completely by yourself. It looks so neat and even. What a great job! I hope you feel proud."

Christine has mastered a new skill. She has a sense of pride and accomplishment. And, as with everything you will

---

Figure 7.1

Shaping a Behavior

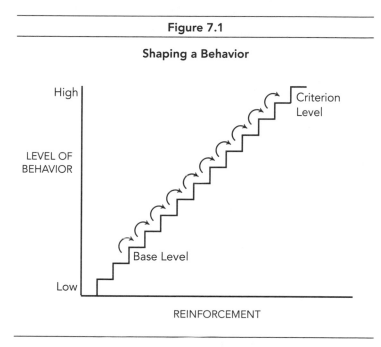

learn in the CSP, you can require her to do this every morning forever, meaning there is one less thing for you to do.

There is no limit to what you can teach your child, regardless of whether she is labeled ADD/ADHD (IA/HM). As she grows older, teach her to cook, sew, fix a light switch, and drive a car. It will make your child self-assured and independent. Stop doing everything for her and teach her to do many things for herself.

Apply the principle of shaping to her schoolwork. If she is having difficulty with a skill, break it down into small steps and use shaping. Once she learns an academic skill, you will require her to do it by herself, without you sitting next to her all the time.

For example, let's look at shaping a writing skill. We'll try the letter "L" in cursive. Christine's "L" looks like:

Teach her the upper loop—Step 1.

Reinforce.
Then the back of the letter:

Reinforce.
Finally, the lower loop:

Reinforce.
And the job is done.

A good schoolteacher uses shaping throughout the academic day with all her students. By walking around the room, she can teach those children who are having difficulty a new small step and reinforce them. She can help improve each child at the particular step where each one is, and each child becomes a winner at the end of the school day.

There is absolutely nothing physically wrong with ADD/ADHD (IA/HM) children, and there is nothing they can't learn. Accept this principle and watch it actually happen. Both you and your child will feel great.

Andrew

At the time of this writing, Andrew is nine years old. His parents came for help with him when he was seven. He was a terror, a full-blown ADD/ADHD (IA/HM) child. At home, he yelled and screamed and played in a wild, out-of-control manner, throwing toys around at will. Neither parent could control him. They dreaded taking him to a store, especially the grocery store. If they turned their backs for a second, he'd ram the grocery cart into someone. They were constantly telling him "No!" and slapping the back of his hand. Nothing fazed this child. In school, he frequently called out, left his seat to roam around the room, never completed his work, and was often caught with items stolen from other children.

Andrew's parents were trained in the CSP, and in less than four weeks after completing training, he was well behaved at home and at school. I asked the parents to train Andrew in helping with the housework. At first they looked puzzled. They said they were satisfied just to have some peace and quiet. But I continued to encourage them to do more, and finally they decided to give it a try. The first week they used shaping to teach him to make his bed and set the dinner table. He loved it. He felt proud and frequently asked if he was doing a good job. The following week they used shaping to help him clean the dinner table and load the dishwasher. Again, he loved it. He beamed at the praise, the feeling of sharing, and the increased responsibilities. Soon he learned to use kitchen knives to help with dinner preparation, a major symbolic step for him as a sign of maturity and responsibility. His dad was so surprised at his progress that a few weeks later he asked Andrew if he'd like to learn to use some of the tools in the garage and help with his woodworking hobby. Andrew was wonderful. Helping his dad to build things became a special avenue for bonding. The two grew closer and closer.

Without any formal intervention, Andrew's schoolwork improved dramatically. He actually started making honors and was a favorite source of positive gossip among the teachers. He was earning praise everywhere, and he became a happy and highly self-motivated child.

Andrew now helps his dad repair the family car, and his mother reports that when Andrew and his dad are in the garage, they are serious. Their verbal exchanges are soft and businesslike. "Son, can you pass me the Phillips?" Andrew asks, "What size?" Dad replies, and hour by hour they work together. Reinforcement now takes a less overt form. Dad doesn't say much; the beaming pride on his face (remember, just showing a reaction is a reinforcement) says it all. Dad and Andrew love to go to baseball games together, and sometimes Mom goes. She now says that she can hardly remember what Andrew used to be like. He constantly wants to learn new skills. She says, "He's just an all-around great kid." He now has a baby sister, and he is fully trusted to hold her, feed her, and change her. That is a lot of responsibility and trust for a nine-year-old.

In the next chapter, we'll begin to understand all aspects of punishment and discipline. We will learn why certain punishments not only fail to work but can actually make matters worse for the ADD/ADHD (IA/HM) child. We'll learn precisely how to discipline effectively.

CHAPTER 8

Why Punishment Fails and Discipline Works

D ID YOU EVER CONSIDER that the meaning of punishment is different from that of discipline? In fact, there are many differences. We're going to explore them and find out what it really takes to control the ADD/ADHD (IA/HM) child.

PUNISHMENT VERSUS DISCIPLINE

Punishment involves doing something specifically painful to a child. In parenting, this usually means hitting and yelling. On the other hand, discipline means using consequences that do not hurt the child, but effectively control his or her behavior. Discipline involves either the loss of reinforcement or the application of boredom. The methods that qualify as discipline here are Ignoring, Time Out, and Reinforcement Removal.

Let's look at several reasons punishment not only doesn't work well, but actually can make matters worse for ADD/ADHD (IA/HM) children, and the reasons discipline does work.

1. *Punishment makes a child nervous.*
   Discipline doesn't make a child nervous.
   If our goal is to teach the ADD/ADHD (IA/HM) child new behaviors, then making him nervous defeats that purpose. A nervous child doesn't learn. He will repeat the same mistakes over and over again. A nervous child also stands an excellent chance of developing emotional problems. There are two basic cornerstones in psychology that underlie most neurotic behaviors—nervousness or anxiety and depression. A child who is habitually punished will become an emotional wreck. With properly designed discipline we don't have the problem of nervousness.

2. *Punishment trains a child to tune out her environment.*
   Discipline doesn't cause a child to tune out her environment.
   If you yell at or hit your child, then you are training her to tune you out. Over time, you will have to yell louder and hit harder in order to get any responses from her. You're actually training or shaping your child to be ADD/ADHD (IA/HM). The hallmark of the ADD/ADHD (IA/HM) child is that she tunes out and doesn't pay attention to her environment. Thus, punishment actually makes her worse.

   Proper discipline doesn't cause a child to tune out.

In fact, it makes her think about what she did wrong and how she affected other people.

3. *Punishment teaches a child to be aggressive.*
   Discipline doesn't teach aggression at all.
   When you yell at or hit your child, you are modeling how you handle your frustrations. You're teaching your child to be aggressive. He is learning to yell and hit from your example. Is it any wonder that ADD/ADHD (IA/HM) children often get into scuffles with other children when they are picked on? Remember: If you hit, they'll hit. If you yell, they'll yell. Since discipline doesn't involve any physical altercations, your child won't be learning to be aggressive.

4. *Punishment causes deep and prolonged, seething anger that will come back to haunt you.*
   Discipline minimizes resentments and builds respect.
   If you hit and yell, the odds are that your child is keeping an emotional or mental scorecard. When she becomes a teenager and discovers her own power, watch out. She'll take out her years of pain on you. With discipline, the child doesn't particularly like the negative consequences, but she understands it's for a particular misbehavior. It doesn't shame her as a person, and she doesn't build a storehouse of resentments.

Johnny

When Johnny was ten, I saw him and his father as patients. Dad was brutal. He'd get mad at Johnny over the slightest thing, yelling and cursing at him. He'd say things like, "You're the dumbest piece of sh-t God ever made!" "Isn't there anything you can do right?" At times he'd slap Johnny across the face. I worked individually with his father for a long time, but nothing changed. He continued to have a hair-trigger temper.

Johnny wasn't aggressive at that time, but at age thirteen he started becoming a bully. He deliberately picked on other kids at school. Sometimes he extorted money from them by threatening to beat them. During this time, his father increased his brutish behavior with Johnny, mostly as a result of phone calls from teachers reporting Johnny's problems. At age fifteen, arguments between Johnny and his father would change to fistfights, and Johnny was big enough to fight back.

I hadn't seen either of them in several years when the father made contact to get help for his out-of-control son. When I saw Johnny, I was shocked. He had long, greasy hair, wore a leather jacket, and had several tattoos, of knives and swastikas. He told me he hated his father, he hated school, and he hated most of the other kids. He described himself as a loner. Johnny looked as if he'd been taking drugs, which he acknowledged, with pot being his favorite.

One evening Johnny waited at home for his father. When the door opened, Johnny swung a long metal pipe right into his father's face. He beat his dad mercilessly, but his dad didn't die. Johnny told me he deliberately aimed the blows away from the head, so as not to kill his dad. Johnny was arrested and received probation, with the stipulation that he continue to see me for counseling.

Several months later, Johnny was arrested for beating another teenager with a pool cue at a pool hall. The other young man was hospitalized, and Johnny was sent to a reform school, where he is now. I believe Johnny will most likely learn to be a career criminal from his time spent in juvenile custody, and someday he'll probably kill someone. His father taught him only too well.

5. *Punishment causes the child to focus on the punisher.*
Discipline helps the child focus on the misbehavior.
When you yell at or hit your child, does he look at you with hate in his eyes? He isn't focusing on what he did wrong; he is focusing his anger on you, the source of his pain. Under these conditions, he isn't learning anything; he is only hating.

With discipline, he can focus on his misbehavior, remember what he did wrong, and think about correcting himself. These are very important goals in working with the ADD/ADHD (IA/HM) child.

6. *Punishment is humiliating.*
Discipline doesn't humiliate.
As a parent you are taking care of your child's soul. If you constantly hit and yell at him, then you are destroying that soul. Being hit and yelled at is humiliating and embarrassing. It produces feelings of shame.

The ADD/ADHD (IA/HM) child engenders negative reactions in almost everyone around him. He already doesn't feel good about himself. Punishing him only adds to this low self-esteem.

Properly designed discipline shouldn't humiliate, degrade, embarrass, or shame a child. With proper discipline he can stop the misbehaviors and at the same time keep his soul and dignity intact.

7. *Punishment actually reinforces undesired behaviors.*
Discipline removes any chance of inadvertent reinforcement.
Recall our list of the components of social reinforcement in chapter 7. If you look carefully at the list, you'll

notice that hitting and yelling actually involve six out of eight elements for reinforcing a behavior.

Components of Social Reinforcement	Present?	
	Yes	*No*
Paying attention to	X	
Looking at	X	
Touching	X	
Talking to	X	
Listening to		X
Spending time with	X	
Praising		X
Showing a reaction	X	

Have you ever noticed that when you constantly yell at or hit the ADD/ADHD (IA/HM) child day after day, he keeps repeating the same behaviors? Remember that any behavior that is maintained or increased is in some way getting reinforced. Now as you look at this list, do you clearly see how punishment is actually reinforcing and maintaining the very misbehaviors that you want to eliminate in the ADD/ADHD (IA/HM) child? Therefore, punishment is very self-defeating. Discipline removes all sources of reinforcement and can't reinforce the misbehaviors.

Scott

When seven-year-old Scott came to my office with his parents, he was all over the room, touching things on my desk, pulling books off the shelves, looking at them, then dropping them on the floor, and finally heading toward my computer. His dad kept telling him to stop this and that, then he started yelling and he smacked Scott on the bottom. Each incident caused the misbehaviors to stop for a minute or two, but inevitably Scott resumed his escapades. I told the father that his punishment methods were actually reinforcing Scott's misbehaviors, but he and Scott's mother didn't believe me at first. After completing the CSP and getting Scott under control, their opinion changed. At the last session, Dad said, "Dr. Stein, I thought what you said at the first session, about reinforcing the behaviors, was bull. I don't feel that way now. We've learned a lot and what you taught us worked. We can't argue with results. If the friends who referred us hadn't been through the program and convinced us to stay, I probably wouldn't have."

8. *Children may seek punishment.*
   Children hate discipline.
   Many years ago we learned that a complete absence of sensory stimulation is perhaps the most aversive condition to humans. If I placed you on a soft white mattress, covered your hands and feet with white cotton, and surrounded you with white walls and a white ceiling, at first you would feel peace and calm. However, within twenty-four hours you would go stark, raving mad. You would do anything to have something titillate your senses. This absence of any input, or zero stimulation, is very aversive. Sometimes it is referred to as sensory deprivation. Children avoid zero stimulation like the plague. They hate it. It's more awful to them than punishment.

   If you look at the three basic forms of stimulation:

Positive	*Zero*	*Negative*
+	0	-

you will notice something interesting. If a child is not receiving positive stimulation, which is reinforcement, and if he avoids zero stimulation at all cost, where must he go for stimulation? Right directly to the negative forms of stimulation that are punishment. I hope you are beginning to learn how and why children function as they do.

THE IMPORTANCE OF ZERO STIMULATION

Psychologists can play dirty. We have learned to use the information about zero stimulation in dealing with children. Several techniques apply zero stimulation, also called boredom, for disciplining undesirable behaviors. The three techniques are Ignoring, Time Out, and Reinforcement Removal.

Ignoring is just about useless with ADD/ADHD (IA/HM) children, so we needn't discuss that. Time Out is quite useful, but currently used approaches aren't designed specifically to deal with the ADD/ADHD (IA/HM) child. I've spent years redesigning Time Out for the ADD/ADHD (IA/HM) child, and I'll be instructing you in its proper use. Reinforcement Removal is particularly useful for dealing with more tenacious behaviors, such as aggression and lying.

TIME OUT AVOIDS THE PITFALLS OF PUNISHMENT

Time Out is a form of discipline that avoids the pitfalls of punishment. The benefits of correctly using Time Out are listed below:

1. No pain
2. No nervousness
3. No tuning out the environment
4. No teaching or modeling of aggression
5. No prolonged and deep-rooted anger within the child
6. The child focuses on the behavior instead of the punisher
7. No humiliation or degradation of the child
8. No inadvertently reinforcing misbehaviors
9. No stimulation-seeking behaviors
10. Zero stimulation—Time Out is thoroughly BORING.

In the next chapter we'll thoroughly review all the steps and components of Time Out specifically designed for the ADD/ADHD (IA/HM) child. If you've tried Time Out and it didn't work, don't worry: That's what I would expect. Currently popular approaches are not carefully designed for ADD/ADHD (IA/HM) children. Not only do they not work, they make matters worse. Let's go on to learn how you can truly get results.

CHAPTER 9

Time Out for

ADD/ADHD (IA/HM)

I N THIS CHAPTER we're going to learn how to use Time Out as it is specifically designed for controlling the child diagnosed as ADD/ADHD (IA/HM). You'll find that the method described here is particularly rigorous. If you enforce Time Out carefully, however, using each of the rules described here, you'll find that your child will make dramatic changes within two weeks. As new, appropriate behavior patterns emerge, the need to use Time Out will quickly disappear, and instead you'll be reinforcing your child abundantly. Other children and other adults will begin to like your child, and they will treat him much more positively. Your child's schoolwork will improve, and so will his self-esteem. If done correctly, you will see a better-behaved, more successful, happier child.

THE RULES FOR TIME OUT FOR THE ADD/ADHD (IA/HM) CHILD

Time Out means time out from all reinforcement. Think of it as the application of pure boredom as a consequence of any of the Target Behaviors. It is a form of zero stimulation, or sensory deprivation. *If carried out correctly*, it is the most highly effective method of discipline known, and it has none of the side effects of punishment. It is essential that you follow each rule. If you don't, you will not get rapid and optimal results. Remember, I've designed these rules specifically to deal with the ADD/ADHD (IA/HM) child.

RULE 1 — THE CHAIR

Find a large, comfortable chair that you can designate as the Time Out chair. Hardback chairs are uncomfortable, and discomfort is not the purpose of Time Out. Sofas are too easy to stretch out on and fall asleep. It is best if the chair is not near a window. Looking out can be reinforcing. If this isn't practical, just keep the blinds closed.

RULE 2 — NO REINFORCERS NEAR THE CHAIR

Make certain that any objects the child could play with aren't near the chair. Coasters can be flying saucers, and pens can be rocket ships. There should be no reading materials near the chair.

Make certain that nothing is visible from the chair that can provide entertainment. For one family I worked with,

Time Out wasn't working until Dad sat in the chair and realized he could see and hear the TV at the end of a long hallway. Moving the chair two feet away from the hallway made the difference, and things began to improve.

It is best to use a lightly trafficked room. Watching lots of activity is too entertaining, that is, reinforcing. A completely empty room makes it too easy for your child to hear you coming to check on her. Formal living rooms usually work well for the Time Out chair.

Make certain that the room is well lit. Darkness often induces sleep.

Do not face the chair toward a wall. That's degrading and unnecessary. Never embarrass or humiliate your child when enforcing Time Out.

A child's bedroom is not a good choice for Time Out. There are too many things to play with. Merely looking at a toy can foster imagination.

Rule 3 — Do Not Use a Bathroom for Time Out

I have this as a separate rule because several books I've read actually recommend using bathrooms for Time Out. Not only are there many things to play with in this room, but a bored child will also explore, and there are too many dangerous things, like pills and razors, to find. This is a completely unsatisfactory choice for Time Out.

Rule 4 — No Clocks

There should be no clocks visible from the Time Out chair. You want your child to lose all track of time. Try an easy exercise. Have someone time you while you sit in the Time Out chair for ten minutes. I promise you it will seem like an eternity when you have no way of telling the time.

You should have a timing device for yourself. I use an inexpensive watch that I can set for the requisite time and that beeps when time is up. If you don't have a timer for yourself, you will get distracted and forget you put your child in Time Out. Hours may go by before you remember. I'll confess it's happened to me more than once. Make certain that when the timer beeps it's not audible to your child. If she's been misbehaving, the beep will cue her to act perfectly only just before she is to come out. You want her to be well behaved for the entire time while in Time Out.

Rule 5 — The Minimum Time in Time Out

The following are the minimum amounts of time in Time Out that work best:

Age	Minimum Time
3 to 4	3 minutes
4 to 5	5 minutes
5 to 11	10 minutes

Researchers have recommended many variations of Time Out times, but those shown above work best with ADD/ADHD (IA/HM) children. Remember these are the minimum times. Under no circumstances should children come out earlier.

RULE 6 — THE MAXIMUM TIME IN TIME OUT

Life! Well, theoretically it can be life. Your child is not to come out of Time Out if he is misbehaving in any way. His behavior must be perfect when the minimum time is reached, or he stays in until he behaves perfectly. No crying, whining, begging, pleading, whistling, singing, humming, or sitting upside down is permitted. He stays in until he is behaving perfectly, then clock one minute of perfect behavior before telling him to come out. For example, if Billy is crying at the ten-minute mark, leave him in there. If he stops at the sixteenth minute, clock one minute extra of silence, and then tell him to come out.

Do not tell him or remind him to behave correctly in order to come out. Leave him in there. He'll know the rules. As soon as you say something to him, you'll be reinforcing his misbehavior. Never, never, never talk to your child while he is in Time Out. This is a major feature for dealing with ADD/ADHD (IA/HM) children. If you say, "Johnny, if you'd stop crying, I'd let you out," you will not get results

This gives you a glimpse of how rigorous the CSP must be. Remember, this is designed for the ADD/ADHD (IA/HM) child who won't listen to orders and who refuses to behave correctly. Do not be afraid to be strict.

Keep your child in Time Out even if it initially takes her hours to quiet down. While this is rare, it has occurred. If you stay firm, within a few days she'll get the idea and behave correctly whenever she has to go to Time Out. For many families, the average time during the first few days is twenty-one minutes. The longest I've seen is four hours, but that was for only four children in my twenty-five-year career.

Rule 7 — Bottom on the Chair Rule

At no time is his bottom to come out of the chair. Once commanded to go to Time Out, he must go immediately or his bottom is considered out of the chair. For being out of the chair he receives a spanking that consists of three solid smacks on the behind, never elsewhere. Repeat this no more than three times in a given day. If you don't spank hard enough, it will fail, and you'll be spanking him every day for the rest of his life. *The purpose of the spanking is to train him to stay in Time Out, and hopefully you will never have to spank again.* Usually, telling him that this will happen is sufficient to avoid the spanking.

We talked earlier about punishment and all its negative side effects. Spanking is a rarely used backup. If rarely used, it can be effective, and the goal is never to use it, if possible. There are only two times spanking is ever appropriate: training your child to stay in Time Out, and when he does something very dangerous, such as running into the street without looking. If you never have to spank, I'll be happy.

If spanking your child doesn't train her well to stay in the chair, there is an additional backup procedure. If you are completely against spanking, then you can choose to use this technique. Empty her room of all toys, playthings, and reinforcers. Put a one-way peephole in the door, to observe for safety. Put two locks on the outside of her door, one at the top and one at the bottom for stability—a simple slide-bolt-type lock will do. She has a choice: go directly to Time Out immediately or go into the room. Once she is in the room, carry out all the rules. Do not delay or hesitate to follow through quickly and efficiently.

Rule 8 — Go on Verbal Command

Your child should go to Time Out "faster than a speeding bullet" when you say, "Go to Time Out!" Do not tell her why. If you do, you're interacting with her and reinforcing her behavior. Do not physically put her in, which is also reinforcing. Make allowances for the three-year-olds, however: You can put them in. But after age four, if they don't go immediately on command, their bottom is out of the chair, and then they get spanked.

Rule 9 — No Warnings

Never give a warning. Never count "1-2-3 Time Out." This will violate everything we are trying to do with the ADD/ADHD (IA/HM) child.

If you warn him, he'll become reliant on you as a "reminder machine." Yes, you probably will get him to comply with the warning, but he will not remember what to do the next day and the day after. *Getting him to remember is an essential part of the training in the CSP and a major change from current programs.*

Remember our discussion on Cognitive/Behavioral Dependency. A warning fosters his dependency on your reminders to help him behave. We want him to remember how he should behave, on his own. He doesn't have some mysterious disease that prevents him from doing this. Enforce the rule, and you'll soon reject these disease theories, and you'll soon see that your child can and will remember.

165

Rule 10 — No Bargaining

Once you say, "Go to Time Out," do not back down. If she says, "All right, Mommy, I'll pick up my toys," do not bargain. She must go to Time Out immediately.

If you bargain with her, you are teaching her to test how far she can go to get away with misbehaving. Testing parents is a trademark of ADD/ADHD (IA/HM) children. You must be very firm if you want to get results with the CSP. *Do not back down.*

Rule 11 — Immediacy

Enforce Time Out immediately when a misbehavior or Target Behavior occurs. She will learn to associate the Time Out with the misbehavior when the consequences occur right after the behavior.

Rule 12 — Time Out at the Mere Hint of a Misbehavior

At the mere hint of a misbehavior, send your child to Time Out. This will make him acutely aware of his behaviors and help him remain vigilant about his conduct at all times.

If you say, "Billy, please pick up your toys," and he turns away from you, without hesitation say, "Go to Time Out!" Or if his face shows that he's getting mad and he has a Target Behavior of temper tantrums, tell him to go to Time Out.

If you're going to err, then err on the side of toughness. You must establish yourself as the boss. This disease nonsense has prevented too many parents from taking control, and it has resulted in too many children being put on amphetamines. Always remember the benefits. By being tough, you keep them off the drugs, they become well behaved, and they receive lots of hugs, kisses, and praises. This, too, is a major difference between the CSP and other programs, and it's a must for the ADD/ADHD (IA/HM) child.

RULE 13—NEVER TALK TO YOUR CHILD WHILE HE OR SHE IS IN TIME OUT

I mentioned this earlier, but it is so important I am emphasizing it as a rule. Once your child is in Time Out, say nothing to him. Never say, "If you'd stop whining you'd get out!" Once you say anything, you reinforce his misbehavior, and he'll wind up staying in longer. By talking to him, you'll neutralize the effectiveness of Time Out. Say nothing.

RULE 14—NEVER PHYSICALLY PUT HIM IN TIME OUT AND NEVER PHYSICALLY TAKE HIM OUT— HE GOES ON VOICE COMMAND

If you physically put your child in Time Out, you'll be inadvertently reinforcing his misbehavior. Your physical involvement causes lots of social reinforcement. Your interaction with him at the time of a misbehavior should be minimal, nothing more than "Go to Time Out" or "Come out of Time Out." Remember the rule: He goes to Time Out on voice command.

With a three-year-old some guiding and helping will be necessary. After age four, he can learn to go in and out on his own.

Rule 15 — "Why Did You Go to Time Out?"

When she is in Time Out, your child must think about what she did wrong. Do not remind her or instruct her over this issue each time she goes in. After you've explained the rules to her initially, she'll know what she must remember.

After you say, "Come out of Time Out" and she comes to you, then say, "Why did you go to Time Out?" If she knows, then tell her to do the correct behavior. If she can't remember what she did wrong, tell her, "Go back to Time Out." Now you are about to learn an interesting lesson about child psychology. She may put on one terrific performance of being totally unable to tell you what she did wrong. And, believe me, these children can be convincing. The second time she comes out, she'll tell you precisely what she did wrong. I can't tell you how many parents I've heard say, "Why, that little bugger knew all along!" *Training ADD/ADHD (IA/HM) children to remember is a crucial component for the success of the CSP.*

Repeat only a third time. If she still can't tell you, then she is genuinely confused and you should just tell her yourself.

It's OK to tell a three-year-old what she did wrong after she comes out of Time Out. She's a little too young to remember on her own. Most children are able to remember by age four.

RULE 16 — REQUIRING PERFORMANCE OF THE CORRECT BEHAVIOR

After he tells you what he did wrong, he's required to do the correct behavior. Immediately! For example, "Johnny, why did you go to Time Out?" "Because I didn't pick up my toys when you asked me." "Good, now what should you do?" "Pick them up." "Please do it now." "Yes, ma'am." And he then does it. Reinforce him as soon as he complies.

If there is any hesitation or a hint of defiance, send him back in to Time Out immediately. If you want the ADD/ADHD (IA/HM) patterns to stop, be tough. This toughness is another important feature of the CSP. Treating these children as diseased and unable to function is a major reason other programs fail.

RULE 17 — ABSOLUTE CONSISTENCY

In order to work successfully with the ADD/ADHD (IA/HM) child, the practice of *consistency* must be near perfect. Consistency must apply for the use of Time Out in all locations and among all caregivers.

Whichever parent or caregiver is with the child must apply Time Out with equal rigor. If one parent is enforcing Time Out correctly and the other isn't, you will not get results. If Grandmother cares for your child after school each day and she fails to be consistent, you will not get results. If a teenage sister has the responsibility of caring for your son and she isn't given the authority or training to consistently use Time Out, you will not get results. If you tell your son, "Wait till Dad gets home," you will not get results. Everyone who cares for your child must be consistent.

In chapter 10 we'll discuss the role of the teacher as a caregiver. It would be ideal if all teachers followed the CSP in the classroom, but as yet they haven't been trained to deal with ADD/ADHD (IA/HM) children at this rigorous level. It is my hope that these methods will be included in the classroom management training as an alternative to amphetamines. Ideally, parents and teachers should do the same things.

Consistency also means to use Time Out in all locations: restaurants, malls, grocery stores, family gatherings, and everywhere. Try to spot a convenient place for Time Out should it become necessary. A bench in the mall or an empty table at a restaurant serves well. If nothing convenient is available, use the backseat of your car, but not in hot or bad weather conditions. Stay with your child. Never leave her alone. Turn your back and lean on the car. Carry out the same procedures as if you were home.

If you are a guest at someone's house, use a chair in a bedroom for Time Out. Ask your daughter to come to you and softly whisper to her to go into the bedroom where all the coats are and sit on a chair or bed for Time Out.

Whenever using Time Out in a public place, carry out procedures as quietly and unobtrusively as possible. Try to avoid humiliating or embarrassing your child. However, if he chooses to scream and cry, then let his embarrassment be his problem. Carry out everything as if you were at home. Just before my daughter Heidi turned four, her mother and I decided it was time to improve her behavior at restaurants, and we used Time Out just as I prescribe here. She had a long, continuous tantrum in the restaurant. I gave the waiter a 50 percent tip because I thought he'd have a nervous breakdown! After that evening, Heidi's behavior was so improved that taking her to restaurants was never again a problem. Her mother and I were forever thankful.

Rule 18 — Comprehensiveness

Another major feature of the CSP is to work on *all* Target Behaviors. Don't allow any Target Behavior, or even the mere hint of one, to slip past you. This will ensure that your child will always pay attention to his behaviors and will always remember to try to behave correctly. He will soon learn that if he relaxes his vigilance, discipline immediately follows.

Rule 19 — Misbehaving on the Way to Time Out

What if Johnny kicks a chair or mutters a curse word on the way to Time Out? When the time is up ask him what he did wrong, and then ask, "What did you do on the way to Time Out? Go back!" Start timing from scratch. When he comes out ask, "Why did you go to Time Out a second time?" "What were you supposed to do in the first place? Go do it!"

Rule 20 — Sibling Fights

If a sibling quarrel has gotten out of hand and one of the siblings hasn't withdrawn to her room, then send them both to separate Time Out chairs in separate rooms. Never ask, "What's going on here?" You'll be thoroughly confused as they both unravel tales of how the other started it.

If you directly observed who started it, then you can send that child alone to Time Out.

Rule 21 — "I Have to Go to the Bathroom"

If she says she has to go to the bathroom, send her instead to Time Out. If she can hold it eight hours at night, she can hold it ten minutes in Time Out. If she has an accident, she must clean it up.

For three-year-olds, let them go to the bathroom first, and then start Time Out.

Rule 22 — Reinforce Correct Behaviors

If you fail to actively, immediately, and consistently reinforce, that is, praise correct behaviors, nothing will work. Reinforcement is the true key to success.

Reinforce your daughter *before* she does something wrong. If you're not getting success with your ADD/ADHD (IA/HM) child within two weeks, you're doing one of two things: You're either not using Time Out correctly, as outlined here, or you are not reinforcing correct behaviors frequently enough or with sufficient enthusiasm. *Lack of success is not because your child won't respond; it's because you're doing something incorrectly.*

The Behavioral Burst

This is actually *Rule 23*, but it is so important that it requires a highlighted section. If you are using Time Out correctly, you can expect a full-blown behavior burst for as much as three to five days. This is where all Target Behaviors get worse, possibly much worse, and your child engages in misbehaviors he's never done before. In other words, "all hell will break loose." Stay tough. Do not despair. Your child is like a fish fighting to get free. He is searching for any loophole he can find. If there are no loopholes, then around the fourth or fifth day he'll behave almost perfectly. It's like a miracle unfolding, and it happens that quickly.

Still, do not relax. Do not feel satisfied enough to lighten up. Stay just as tough and as reinforcing as ever. In fact, because he begins to behave well you should find yourself reinforcing a great deal of the time. Days should go by when Time Out isn't necessary.

If the behavioral burst doesn't occur immediately, it sometimes emerges a few weeks later. You can expect it.

EXPLAIN TIME OUT

In the CSP, Time Out is explained only two times—the night before starting the program and the next night. *It is the ADD/ADHD (IA/HM) child's responsibility to remember the rules.*

The explanation should be kept fairly simple. The following are the essential elements:

1. He will go to Time Out for ten minutes. If he misbehaves in Time Out, he will stay in no matter how long, until he behaves correctly. There will be no reminders to behave correctly. No crying, whining,

pleading, or playing with anything will be permitted. It will be up to him to remember.

2. Whenever he goes to Time Out, he must think about what he did wrong. If he can't remember, then he'll be sent back to Time Out. He'll go to Time Out for any and all misbehaviors. Do not review the Target Behaviors, or he'll continually insist that "You didn't tell me that!" He'll learn.

   Do not tell him to think about what he did wrong each time he goes to Time Out. It is a standard rule that *he* must remember. *Actively remembering all the rules is what we want him to do.*

3. If he doesn't go immediately to Time Out, he'll receive a hard spanking. If he gets out of the chair, he'll be spanked.

Keep the explanation this simple. Have your child repeat the explanation and correct any misunderstandings. After the first two nights, never reexplain again.

Do not be dismayed by how he acts at the time of the explanation. Some children laugh in a mocking way, some cry, and some get angry. It doesn't matter: They will soon hate Time Out.

COMMON MISTAKES

The most common mistakes parents make include:

1. not reinforcing enough
2. letting testing behaviors slip by; waiting too long to enforce Time Out

3. giving warnings
4. inconsistency between Mom and Dad
5. not using Time Out for all Target Behaviors
6. being softhearted.

By now you realize how strict the CSP is. It is essential to keep in mind that allowing your child to continue to act as an ADD/ADHD (IA/HM) child will condemn her to failing in school, being ostracized and picked on by other children, and not learning to function in an independent way. It also means keeping her on amphetamines for an indeterminate period of time, possibly even into adulthood, with all the inherent risks of those drugs.

The sooner you get her under control, the more close and loving your relationship can become.

In the next chapter, we'll learn how to deal with school problems should they persist. Remember that for 80 percent of the ADD/ADHD (IA/HM) children who have been parented by the CSP, school automatically gets better. If it doesn't, which happens 20 percent of the time, you will find that the next chapter will tell you the additional steps of the CSP for school problems.

Do not begin the school program until everything is well under control at home. Allow about one month to see if school improves without further intervention.

CHAPTER 10

Improving School Performance for the ADD/ADHD (IA/HM) Child

After two months of implementing the CSP, all Target Behaviors should be *completely* under control, except perhaps school conduct and performance. If all Target Behaviors are not completely under control at home, it will be futile to attempt school intervention. Whenever a family has had difficulty getting complete improvement, I carefully review everything they are doing in order to detect any flaws in their application of the CSP. I almost always can find them and help with the necessary corrections. Obviously, I can't do that with each reader here. Therefore, I recommend two steps. The first is to review all the stages of the CSP and try to identify where you may be making mistakes. Review the most common mistakes in the previous chapter. If you are unable to find the problem, then try asking a third party, such as a friend, to read this book and have him or her observe what you are doing. You'd be surprised how an objective third party can help detect mistakes.

Remember that after achieving excellent results with the CSP, 80 percent of my cases demonstrate improvement in school conduct and performance. If you are in the remaining 20 percent, don't despair. In this chapter we're going to discuss the specific steps you can take to get all school problems under control.

Resolving Two Important Issues

There is an important issue we must address before starting the school program. This involves your attitude and your ADD/ADHD (IA/HM) child's attitude toward education and reading. How strongly do both of you value education and reading?

VALUING EDUCATION

A child who deeply loves and treasures learning will never become diagnosed as ADD/ADHD (IA/HM). If parents do not actively instill a love for learning and a deep appreciation for education, their child will not take school seriously and will not be *motivated* to perform well there.

Learning requires lots of energy, sustained attention, avid interest, active reading and listening, hard memorizing, and deep concentration. These are difficult things for a child to do. To master these skills, your child must be highly motivated.

There are several steps you can take to make learning and education exciting and important to your child. Love of learning is a value, or deep belief. Our values and beliefs mediate how we behave. How can you get your child to cherish learning deeply?

1. Make it a *daily* practice to show an active interest in your child's schoolwork. Show your pleasure when he does well. Praise him. Get excited. Reinforce him for his sustained efforts after his seven-hour workday.

   Have a large bulletin board, perhaps in your kitchen, where your child can display excellent test and homework grades and drawings.

   At dinner ask your child how his day went. This shows an active interest on your part, and it demonstrates that you care. Don't assume he knows that you care; it is essential that you show it. Keep dinner conversation at a low-key level. There's no need to be overly exuberant or boisterous. Whatever you do, please *don't lecture*. If he's had a bad day, be an encourager and say, "I'm sorry you didn't do well on your math test, but you are smart. You can do it. If something is confusing, I'll help you clear it up, and then maybe you can practice on your own until you feel sure that you've conquered the problem. You've done this many times before. Do you remember how good you felt when you licked that science problem you had last month?"

2. Take the family on short, fun-filled educational trips. Visit museums, college campuses, and historical places. I'll bet that you live in an area rich with fascinating history that even you may not know. You can learn together.

3. A love for nature can be educational and recuperative. Your and your child's daily lives may be stressful, but few things refresh us as much as a day spent outdoors. Hiking and camping provide exercise as well as induce wonderful feelings of peace and serenity. In addition, learning about nature can be exciting.

  Take trips to scenic places. Go camping and together learn as much as you can about camping skills. Take frequent day hikes. Get up early and watch the sun rise. Invest in a telescope and scan the heavens. Have your child help plant flowers and shrubs. Visit planetariums.

4. Demonstrate a love for music. I love all types of music: rock, pop, country, and classical. It's important that children learn that they can enjoy all varieties and they don't have to limit themselves to rock.

  I believe that live concerts can excite an enthusiasm for music far more than tapes or CDs. If it's within your budget, take your child to all kinds of live concerts, screening out risqué or inappropriate acts. I've often witnessed children turn dislike for classical music into a love for it after attending a live symphony. Fortunately, I live near Colonial Williamsburg, and my children can attend live chamber music recitals. They've grown to love it. If finances are a concern, remember that colleges and universities offer all types of concerts at very cheap rates, and the public is usually welcome.

5. Plays are great fun. Live theater can be a joy for a child. Again, if cost is a consideration, colleges, universities, and even high schools offer inexpensive performances for the public.

   Most cities have theaters devoted exclusively to children's plays. Check the newspapers and yellow pages for availability. I recall taking my daughter, Heidi, at age ten to a production of *To Kill a Mockingbird*. During the trial scene, where a black man was being tried for a crime he didn't commit, the prosecutor began to yell at the man. My daughter suddenly stood up and cried out, "You leave him alone!" Everyone in the cast froze, and the theater went dead silent. All eyes turned to Heidi. Even the actors looked up. After what seemed like an eternity, everyone realized what happened and began to laugh. Heidi quietly sat down, embarrassed, and I hugged her and reassured her. She was okay. Today she is passionate about attending plays. Some communities have free outdoor plays and concerts. Why not take advantage of them?

6. Visit college campuses. Many parents want their children to go to college but they never visit one. Such visits help translate the abstract idea of college to a concrete reality, and many campuses are beautiful. They also offer free guided tours, often filled with lots of local history.

7. Travel. Visit other cities and states. Collect brochures *before* you go. You can get them by mail from the state or city chamber of commerce. Read these brochures together with your child to make the trip more meaningful and fun.

8. Instead of buying a mountain of toys for holidays and birthdays, why not mix in a few educational tools, such as a microscope, chemistry set, ant colony, or magnet set? Most malls now have science, nature, and educational stores that may carry these items.

9. Help your child to develop a hobby. Again, instead of toys for special occasions, consider a train set, wood carving kit, model airplane and boat kits, coin- and stamp-collecting kits, or art supplies. At age twelve, my older son, Alex, expressed an interest in learning photography. I know that once he makes his mind up to master something, he'll do it; so two Christmases ago I invested in a fully manual camera and an introductory book on photography. He stayed up all night reading the manual and used the camera the very next day.

10. Computers are gradually becoming as much a part of the home as telephones and televisions. If you can afford a computer, there are limitless educational opportunities. Searching the Web together to discover information about an endless variety of topics can be a lot of fun. My kids are better at making these searches than I am.

11. Playing games together is an excellent way for families to spend time together, and games can be educational. Consider playing "Scrabble," "Monopoly," "Chess," "Go to the Head of the Class," "Trivial Pursuit," and many more.

12. Limit junk TV to only one hour a night. There are now several channels, however, with shows that convey information in exciting and fun ways. If homework is completed, why not jointly watch shows

about nature, science, and history? I deeply believe that as children adjust to this form of entertainment, they will eventually prefer it to sitcoms and cartoons. Watching educational TV can greatly enhance learning about school topics and can even help make schoolwork more exciting, real, and concrete.

I hope these twelve suggestions help you to make learning and education important values for your child. If your child loves learning, then watch the ADD/ADHD (IA/HM) behaviors disappear.

Loving education requires loving to read. In the next section we'll review how you can help your child develop a love for reading.

INSTILLING A LOVE FOR READING

Reading should be fun. It should be a joy, yet most ADD/ADHD (IA/HM) children do not like to read because to them it's a chore. It's required. It's something *they have to do*. Learning the mechanics of reading is less important than developing a motivation to read. The best way to improve reading is to read. Our job is to get our children to want to read. I'd like to share with you ten helpful hints for reversing your child's attitude and to instill a passion for reading.

10 Ways to Make Reading Fun

1. When children are young, most parents know how important it is to read to them every evening at bed-

time. But sometimes parents are uncertain about how to select materials that are both fun and educational.

If your child loves a particular storybook and wants you to read it *every* night, then by all means do so. At the same time, to expand her repertoire of stories, make a pact with her. Agree to read her favorite story only if she'll let you follow it with a new story. Since most children don't want to go to sleep right away, she'll usually see this as a way to outsmart you and stay awake longer.

By trial and error, pay attention to the kinds of stories she loves, whether they are adventures, mysteries, fairytales, funny stories, or family stories. Choose materials that capture her imagination.

When selecting stories to read to your child, choose those that are at or above her current reading level, not grade level. Reading levels are determined by twice-yearly national reading tests. Ask your child's teacher to explain the score, which is usually reported by grade level. For example, if your child is in the third grade and scores 5.3 on his test, this means that he is reading at the fifth-grade, third-month level. Then you should try to select reading material at the fifth- through seventh-grade levels. If your child scores 2.8, then he is reading at the second-grade, eighth-month level, and you'll want to select second- through fourth-grade books. Bookstores and libraries usually group books by levels. Or you can read the jacket of the book for more information.

The reason I make this suggestion is that most children have excellent auditory or listening skills. This is the time when their brains are ready for learning language, and they learn vocabulary more readily by listening than by looking. Therefore, you'll be introducing them to auditory vocabulary that will improve their familiarity with words and help with word recognition when they learn sight-reading at school. Being familiar with words makes it easier to decipher them when they are introduced in school texts. Helping them develop listening skills also reduces the ADD (IA) component of ADD/ADHD (IA/HM). Encourage them to ask about words they don't understand. And don't select material that is too advanced, because you want this nightly ritual to be FUN.

2. When selecting books for them to read on their own, try to choose ones that are from their current to *lower* levels. Then they won't trip over every other word, and they'll be able to focus more on the content of the story.

   The best way to improve reading skills is to read. If it's easy and fun, they'll read, but if it's difficult, they won't. As children get into the reading habit, their skills will automatically improve.

3. Few children want to go to sleep at bedtime. Rather than engage in a battle of wills every night, why not let them stay up an extra thirty minutes for reading? No other activity, such as drawing or playing with a toy, should be permitted. Bedtime reading is a habit that you want your child to develop early in life. Younger prereaders can adopt this nightly habit by looking at pictures. Make certain that the reading material is at an easy and comfortable level.

4. The library is a special place, and it should be familiar and comfortable for all children. To make this

happen, take frequent trips to the library with your child, at least every other week. Select books to read to her and for her to read by herself. In an effort to please or impress their parents, sometimes children will select material that is too advanced. Tell her that what you really want is that she will have fun with what she reads.

At an early age my son Kevin was selecting very difficult books. His mother discovered that he was trying to impress us and that he didn't understand what he was choosing. We insisted he select easier books. We'd have him read aloud a few passages to be certain it was easy. Kevin is now an avid reader.

Help her select topics she enjoys, but make some effort to help her to expand her interests. Don't push too hard if you meet resistance.

5. Children love to receive mail. Subscribe to children's magazines in your child's name. These magazines often have fun exercises and activities you can do jointly. I think you'll be pleasantly surprised how important the mail becomes to your child.

6. There is a stubborn myth that has been around for years that comic books impair reading skills. This is absolutely not true. If your child loves comics, then go with it. Fun is our central theme. Select the comics with care, however: Some are indeed violence- and sex-oriented.

7. Reading should be a family activity. For an hour or more each evening, turn off the TV and read. You are a role model, and seeing you read conveys the message that it is important.

When my boys and I read together, I usually have one stretched out on the sofa with his head on my lap and the other leaning on my opposite arm. While I sometimes feel cramped, I must admit that for me this is a touch of heaven.

8. If you can afford to purchase books, try to build a small library for your child. Teach him to treasure books.

9. Whenever an opportunity arises for quiet talk with your child, inquire about her reading. Try to avoid pressuring her, but if she seems excited, show your enthusiasm.

10. Fill your home with reading material. Your child will casually pick up and read magazines and books that are readily available.

The goal is to make reading fun. Perhaps the one occasion when noncompliance is a good thing is when your child is so engrossed in reading that he doesn't hear you. If that happens with reasonable frequency, then sigh with relief; you've won—ADD/ADHD (IA/HM) habits have been conquered. If you peek into his bedroom late at night and he's under the cover reading by flashlight, then, again, sigh with relief—you've conquered the ADD/ADHD (IA/HM) habits. The "disease" is in full remission!

THE CSP FOR IMPROVING SCHOOL PERFORMANCE

I want you to reflect on something interesting. If a child misbehaves mildly at home, psychologists call him a misbehaving child, which has no official *DSM-IV* diagnosis. If he misbehaves at home at more severe levels, then he's officially diagnosed as Oppositional/Defiant, which psychologists have not labeled as a disease. However, if a child misbehaves at school, he's labeled as ADD/ADHD (IA/HM).

The *DSM-IV* diagnosis criteria discussed in chapter 4 indicate that the ADD/ADHD diagnosis mainly applies to school performance and conduct. Quite frankly, *ADD/ADHD (IA/HM) children usually hate schoolwork*. They may like being at school to be with their friends, but they hate doing work. ADD/ADHD (IA/HM) is primarily a problem of motivation and not a mysterious disease. Psychologist and educator Mike Valentine (1998) asks a very interesting question: "Why does the disease disappear when the principal walks into the room?"

Our goal in this part of the book is to get your child's school conduct and schoolwork under control. Once under control, it is crucial that you implement as many of the suggestions we covered as possible to change her attitude about learning. This program helps by getting behaviors under control, but the true long-term solution is instilling a love for learning and reading. This is the true cure for ADD/ADHD (IA/HM).

BEFORE BEGINNING THE SCHOOL PROGRAM

Before starting the school program, it is important that you take the following four steps:

1. Have your child's vision and hearing examined. Sometimes vision or hearing problems remain undetected for years. Schedule her for a checkup with the appropriate specialists.

2. Have your child's IQ (Intelligence Quotient) tested. IQ tests do not really measure intelligence—they measure a child's readiness to function in an academic environment. Therefore, I prefer the term RQ, or Readiness Quotient. So as not to confuse the point any further, I'll use the traditional IQ measure.

An IQ of 100 means that a child can perform at the average level for children of the same age and grade. He or she should be able to make Cs and Bs with reasonable effort. With a score of 120, a child should be able to make Bs and As with reasonable effort and should be able to perform well at college.

A child with an IQ of 80 or below will have difficulty keeping pace with a regular class. At lower levels, a child will perhaps perform better in smaller classes that are self-paced, where his progress is not measured by competing with others. Classes where the level of material is matched to a child's ability are usually beneficial and can help considerably in reestablishing motivation and a feeling of success within a child.

3. Make certain your child is tested for any specific learning disabilities, or LDs. These problems involve children with normal or above normal IQ who have difficulty with one or two specific learning skills, such as reading or math.

Undetected LDs make learning difficult and can be the reason a child does not pay attention or misbehaves in class, or is ADD/ADHD (IA/HM). However, the reverse is also true: Inattention for several years can cause the LD problems, because the child then doesn't adequately learn fundamental skills in some subject areas. Actually, the latter is the most common cause of LD problems. In either case, have your child tested.

4. If the ADD/ADHD (IA/HM) problems suddenly emerged, then consider the possibility of problems with a stern teacher or with a school bully terrorizing your child. At times I've also known children to misbehave in order to earn popularity with a particular clique of kids.

IMPLEMENTING A DAILY REPORT CARD

Be sure to maintain control of all Target Behaviors at home. If school doesn't improve, set up a Daily Report Card, shown in Figure 10.1, with your child's teacher(s).

Report cards are usually given every six weeks. This is too long a period of time for effectively shaping behaviors. We need precise information every day in order to match consequences with four categories: (1) class performance, (2) class conduct, (3) test and quiz grades returned each day, and (4) homework grades returned each day.

In the first column, subjects are listed in the order they occur each day. Class performance, in the second column, consists of the teacher's rating for ADD (IA) behaviors in each class: for paying attention when the teacher is speaking; performing assigned tasks properly by keeping their eyes directly on their work; and participating in class with appropriate behavior, such as raising a hand to ask or answer questions instead of calling out. This estimates ADD (IA)–type behavior while in school. A global estimate is rated by the teacher, who writes in E = excellent,

FIGURE 10.1

Daily Report Card

Name: _____

Date: _____

Subjects	Class Performance (Doing work, Participation, and Attention)	Conduct In Class	Tests and Quiz Grades (Returned Today)	Homework Grades (Returned Today)	Teacher's Initials
1.					
2.					
3.					
4.					
5.					
6.					
7.					
8.					
9.					
10.					
11.					
12.					

Comments: _____

_____

_____

_____

E = Excellent
S = Satisfacory
N = Needs Improvement
U = Unsatisfactory

Permission is granted to photocopy for your own use.

S = satisfactory, N = needs some improvement, and U = unsatisfactory or unacceptable.

Class conduct, in the third column, has the teacher estimate the more ADHD (HM)–type behaviors in each class. The teacher globally rates talking out of turn, calling out, throwing spitballs, pushing other children, or any disruptive behaviors. Again, ratings are E, S, N, and U.

The fourth column is for the teacher to record exact grades for each subject for tests or quizzes returned that day. Grading systems vary in scale; in some locales 80 percent is a B, but in others it's a C. Know the grading scale for your child's school.

The fifth column is for the teacher to record precise grades for homework returned that day. Again, be familiar with your school district's grading system.

Finally, the teacher signs her initials after each class.

Es and Ss are considered passing for performance and conduct, and Ns and Us mean failure. Tests, quizzes, and homework are passing only if they are Cs or better, and Ds and Fs are failing.

If even one grade anywhere on the Daily Report Card is a failure, negative consequences are enforced *at home*. The consequences will be covered shortly. The report card serves as a communication tool between the teacher and the parents. The responsibility for discipline is the parents'. This removes the burden of being the disciplinarian from the teacher's shoulders. If the teacher has her own methods for classroom management and discipline, she is free to continue using them. But the parents will carry out appropriate consequences at home and will be the authority.

In the CSP, it is important that the parent stop sitting with the child during homework, though they may serve as a resource for the child's questions or confusions. Let the child struggle with his homework. After consequences are imposed for failing homework grades, you will see his skills finally begin to improve. Remember that sitting with him reinforces his helplessness. Let the Daily Report Card do the work. Your child can function. Expect him to, and he will.

Some parents may protest that discipline for one failing grade in the entire report card is too stern. No, it is not. You've learned that he can behave at home, and now you'll see that he can do his work properly in school and control his conduct there.

Within two to four weeks of enforcing the Daily Report Card, you'll see improvements unfold. Actually, it happens a lot sooner: Often merely beginning the report card, with the child knowing the consequences, is enough to produce results.

I also suggest you use the chart in Figure 10.2. Make a large chart like it and post it on a convenient wall. Have your child post his daily homework and/or test grades for each subject area. The reason for doing this is that children may believe they are doing well based only on the last two grades. This chart serves as a visual reminder of their performance throughout the six-week grading period; when the school's report card is issued, there won't be any surprises.

It is a good idea to have a fixed after-school schedule. I recommend free play for the ADD/ADHD (IA/HM) child from 3:30 to about 5 P.M. This permits her to relax and burn off energy. It also serves as a very important reinforcer. After free play, homework may begin, then perhaps dinner, followed by more homework, perhaps one hour of watching TV, and finally thirty minutes to an hour for quiet family reading. Bedtime should be a set time and

FIGURE 10.2

Record of Test and Homework Grades to Be Posted at Home

Subjects									
Grade									
Date									
Grade									
Date									
Grade									
Date									
Grade									
Date									
Grade									
Date									
Grade									
Date									
Grade									
Date									
Grade									
Date									
Grade									
Date									

Permission is granted to photocopy for your own use.

strictly enforced. At bedtime, I suggest the ritual of quiet talk while you sit next to the bed, perhaps read to the younger children, and finally either thirty minutes of bedtime reading or lights-out.

CONSEQUENCES

If your child has one failing grade, the first level of consequence is the loss of free play only for that day. Your child can decide the next day to get with the program or bear the consequences. Keep this level in effect for one month to see if improvements appear.

Do not permit the substitution of any other activity during loss of free play. Nothing is permitted—no reading, no watching TV, no puzzles or games, no talking on the telephone, no going outside, no helping with dinner preparation, and most important, no doing homework. If she finished her homework during this time, she'd swap time periods and wind up with no meaningful consequences. She must be totally bored. She may walk around the house, but if she does any activity without permission, the remainder of the time is spent in the Time Out chair.

Stay at the level of loss of free play for one month. By then most ADD/ADHD (IA/HM) children will start coming home with passing grades. If yours is a stubborn and recalcitrant child, then add the loss of watching TV. Again, no substitute activities. If this fails after one more month, then go to the next level.

At the third level, if your child fails two days during a week, she gets the daily consequences and she loses all activities for the entire weekend, from Friday at three P.M. to

Monday morning. I've only had a handful of ADD/ADHD (IA/HM) children, out of hundreds of cases in a twenty-five-year career, who ever went to this level. The loss of one weekend is usually sufficient to end school problems. Again, allow no reinforcing activities during the weekend—not even reading. Make it thoroughly boring. I prefer this level of toughness to putting amphetamines in children's bodies.

The Positive Gains

Once your ADD/ADHD (IA/HM) child begins to really function, his whole life will change. He will discover that he can do his work and control his behavior. His self-image will escalate accordingly. His self-confidence will improve. The teachers will reinforce him more with smiles and appreciative looks instead of with dread and condemnation.

Getting good grades is contagious. The more that children get them, the more motivated they are to continue getting good grades; many children decide to go even higher. I've seen that happen many times.

When your child behaves better in all classes, other children will respond more favorably. Better conduct promotes acceptance, which can be very important to a child.

Your frustrations will subside. You'll stop yelling, coaxing, pleading, and begging for her to do better. Instead, you'll be reinforcing with praises and hugs and kisses, and your child will be so much happier. Your stress level and your child's will subside enormously.

Explain the Daily Report Card program only once at the beginning of each new level (if you need to advance to higher levels). Simply tell him the grades he must make and what consequences will occur. Keep your explanation brief and simple. Have him repeat it to you. Correct any misunderstandings and begin the program.

Jay

Jay has been through it all. When I first saw him, he was a nine-year-old third-grade student. He was held over the previous year for failing everything. His parents reported that he'd been a terror ever since they could remember. They began their search for help when he was four.

The first psychologist who saw Jay at that age diagnosed him as ADHD (HM). He recommended a psychiatric evaluation for medication, hinting at a need for Ritalin and play therapy. Dutifully, the parents saw the psychiatrist, who prescribed Ritalin. Jay got worse. After several weeks of Jay's play therapy and Ritalin treatment, the psychologist thought a reevaluation of the medication was in order. The psychiatrist presented a stronger drug, Dexedrine. Jay got even worse. The psychiatrist increased the dosage, which didn't help. After several months, the parents stopped the visits to both the psychologist and the psychiatrist, and they discontinued the medication.

Kindergarten was terrible. Jay disrupted the class constantly. The teacher called the parents at least once or twice each week reporting Jay's misbehaviors. The parents could not get Jay under control, and they said that even at home he was like a nonstop tornado. In the first grade, the teacher demanded an evaluation by the school psychologist and a team meeting, consisting of the assistant principal, the teacher, the school nurse, a guidance counselor, and the school psychologist. In a written report, Jay was diagnosed ADHD (HM), and a psychiatric evaluation was recommended, which is a code for a demand to put him on drugs. Once again, Jay was given Ritalin, and once again his behavior got worse. The dosage of Ritalin was increased, but it seemed to have no effect. After three months, Jay was given Adderall. Again, no change. More time passed. The psychologist put him on a Token Economy program, with rules posted and poker chips given as rewards. When he accumulated chips, Jay could purchase sweets, use toys, or engage in various activities like calling a friend. Nothing changed. He continued to be a one-child destruction machine both at home and at school.

The psychiatrist reevaluated Jay's medication and discontinued the Adderall. He placed Jay on a minor tranquilizer. Jay's behavior didn't change. The dosage was increased twice. At first Jay's behavior slowed down, but he was sleepy all the time. The doctor said this would pass. It did. Jay stopped being sleepy, and his behavior returned to being disruptive. Several different tranquilizers were tried. Nothing changed.

By the third grade, Jay was failing everything, and he could not be controlled. He'd seen two other psychologists. The last one instructed the parents to remind Jay how to behave in all new settings and in every change of environment. While being reminded Jay would nod his head and then quickly proceed to be just as disruptive as ever.

A psychiatrist put Jay on a major tranquilizer called Haldol. Jay developed a muscle contraction in his neck that pulled his head to one side. He developed a hand tremor; he couldn't sit in a chair without immediately getting up; he became restless and agitated. The doctor reassured the parents that these "symptoms" were merely side effects that could be controlled by adding another drug called Cogentin. The bizarre symptoms cleared, but Jay's behavior remained the same. Haldol was discontinued and several other major tranquilizers were tried. Nothing worked. A minor tranquilizer was added. Jay became sleepy and lethargic and could barely walk.

He was put in a psychiatric hospital, where the psychologists tried various behavioral methods while the medications were continued. After one month, the hospital doctors admitted defeat and released him.

Jay failed third grade. It was during his second tenure in the third grade that he began seeing me.

I described to his parents the training they would be going through. I told them they would become semiprofessional behaviorists, because training those people who spent time with Jay would produce the best gains. They readily agreed to the training in the Caregivers' Skills Program and requested that Jay's grandparents attend. While the grandparents didn't serve as primary caregivers, there were frequent arguments within the family over how to parent Jay. I readily consented, with the provision that each adult take individual notes. Grandfather was very recalcitrant; he wasn't going to take notes—that was Grandmother's job. I recommended that he tape-record the sessions and review only those parts where there was confusion between him and his wife. He consented.

Because the family had a history of extreme inconsistency, getting initial improvements took longer than usual. Jay had a three-week behavioral burst; I thought this was one for the record books. However, by the third week Jay began to improve. Within another two weeks, Jay's behaviors

were completely under control, but there was no generalization to school. He was still failing everything. Since Jay
had been tested twice, and both times showed an above-
average IQ and no learning problems, I thought we'd move
ahead on the Daily Report Card program. I wanted Jay's
vision and hearing tested first, and he was found to be very
nearsighted and needed glasses. His hearing was fine. After
he got his glasses, the Daily Report Card program was
implemented when all behaviors at home had been stabilized for one month.

Consequences began with the loss of free play after
school and no substitutions. This phase lasted four weeks,
with no improvement. He continued to fail everything.
The loss of watching TV was added. Four more weeks
went by with no improvement.

We then added the loss of *all* activities for the weekends if he failed two days during the week. Jay could walk
around the house, but nothing else was permitted. If
caught doing an activity he was denied, he'd have to stay in
Time Out. After one weekend, Jay passed all subjects for
participation, conduct, homework, and tests. This began
on Monday and continued through the entire week.
Everyone, especially Jay's teacher, was amazed. I was
thankful the parents had the tenacity to stay tough and
carry out the CSP and the Daily Report Card program
consistently and unhesitatingly.

All this was accomplished without medication. Jay is
now in the seventh grade and doing well. I stopped seeing
him while he was still in the third grade, but I periodically
run into the parents, who tell me how he's doing.

Jay was one of my toughest cases, but his parents were
highly motivated, and that was all that was needed.

GROUNDING DOESN'T WORK

Parents often try grounding, which has no precise meaning. Usually, it involves loss of a favorite activity or object reinforcer for several weeks following a bad six-week report card. This rarely works, for several reasons. First, the child automatically substitutes other reinforcers, for example, loss of the bicycle is replaced with Roller Blading. Second, the length of time for the grounding is too long to help in shaping new behaviors. A child must be given a chance to try new behaviors the very next day after a failure. If he continues to be punished while trying new behaviors, he will feel defeated. Third, whatever reinforcer he's forbidden loses any meaningfulness after a few weeks. He stops caring about losing it. Fourth, as soon as the grounding is stopped, he'll return to his old patterns. In the CSP, with daily enforcement the consequences either go on forever or end the minute he decides to stop behaving like an ADD/ADHD (IA/HM) child.

Now you have plenty of tools to improve his behaviors both at home and at school. I hope you will soon have a happy, well-behaved child. However, we still have more work ahead of us. In the next chapter, we'll deal with aggressive behavior and lying as two more tenacious behaviors to control: it can be done, and we'll learn how. As yet, we haven't dealt with dawdling and that too will be covered.

CHAPTER 11

Targeting Aggression
and Lying

S OMETIMES two of the most tenacious behaviors in
ADD/ADHD (IA/HM) children can be aggression and
lying. Fortunately, they are relatively infrequent. Only a
small percentage of ADD/ADHD (IA/HM) children regularly engage in these Target Behaviors.

Aggression and lying usually dissipate while implementing the CSP, and no further steps are necessary.
However, these are two behaviors that sometimes persist
because they occur less frequently than other Target
Behaviors, and we have fewer opportunities to work on
them. Lying has an additional problem: It is sometimes
very hard to detect.

Younger children usually lie poorly. It's easy to detect
when they're young, and it's best to get this behavior under

control at the earliest possible age. As the child gets older, he becomes a more skillful liar, and your chances for detection become increasingly reduced.

REINFORCEMENT REMOVAL

To add more punch in dealing with aggression and lying, I added the technique called Reinforcement Removal to the CSP. In psychology, it's called response cost, but parents seem to better understand the term Reinforcement Removal, or RR.

This is a relatively easy technique to implement. Simply make a list of at least seven objects or activities that are very important to your son or daughter—a favorite doll, playing video games, bicycle riding, camping, fishing, hunting, favorite CDs, watching a favorite TV show, or use of the telephone. In general, I don't favor material reinforcers in raising children, but an exception is appropriate when trying to get two isolated, difficult behaviors under control. Don't include items on the list that are impractical, such as reading, educational TV shows, or books. Remember to include on the list only items that are reinforcing, or important to your child. If the items aren't important, the program will not work.

Prioritize the list, with item one being the most important and item seven least important. Explain to your child that if he engages in either aggression or lying, he will lose item seven for a very long period of time. You can work on both behaviors simultaneously if your child does them both. Optimal time periods are one week for three- and four-year-olds, one month for five- to seven-year-olds, and one year for eight- to eleven-year-olds. Actually, I've had considerable success using this same technique with teenagers who engage in aggression and/or lying.

These time periods are intended to be strict, because aggression is dangerous and lying is hard to detect. It will help you enforce the program if you keep this in mind.

Write down the starting and ending dates. If you don't, I promise you'll forget.

Tell your child that if she is caught using a withdrawn item, it will be permanently removed. If it is not feasible to permanently remove an item, such as watching TV or using the telephone, then an alternative can be loss of contact with friends for one or even two weeks.

Most children will test the system up to item number three before the aggression and lying stop. A few desist when the parent tells them about the program. Since they've been involved in the CSP, they know the parent means business and will follow through, and the mere threat of this additional program is sufficient. In my career, I had only one child go all the way to item one before he finally quit his aggression. I could devise even more severe disciplines, but I haven't found it necessary. This has sufficed.

Be certain to carefully explain all this to your child before starting. Have him repeat his understanding of the instructions. Clarify any confusion, and then begin. Don't repeat the instructions again; allow the consequences to do the teaching.

George

George, a typical ADHD case with the addition of aggression, was nine years old and misbehaved both at home and at school. The CSP brought all his Target Behaviors under control except his aggression. While he originally had temper tantrums three or four times each week, he became aggressive only about once a month. He went wildly out of control, punching, kicking, and biting whomever he was mad at, whether it was another child or an adult.

A list was made, consisting of:

1. using his Roller Blades
2. using his skateboard
3. playing with his electric trains
4. riding his bike
5. watching TV in his room
6. going to the movies
7. eating sweets

After five aggressive episodes spanning several months, his aggression completely stopped. He had lost items 7 through 3, each for one year. Finally, all Target Behaviors and his aggression were totally controlled.

DAWDLING

Many ADD/ADHD children are dawdlers, especially on school mornings, simply because they hate going. Since Time Out cannot be consistently enforced during the morning rush, a simple change in procedure is called for.

Tell your child that he must be ready by a set time each morning, such as 7:25 A.M. It is his job to remember the rule and be ready on time, not a second later. If he is not, he spends two hours in the Time Out chair immediately after coming home from school. One or two days of this usually ends dawdling as a problem.

Getting a child under control isn't enough. There is more that we must cover, and I ask that you read on. In the next chapter, we'll discuss helping your child to develop better social skills.

CHAPTER 12

Getting Along: Developing Better Social Skills

A T THIS POINT, we've accomplished two important goals: we've gotten *all* Target Behaviors under control, and your ADD/ADHD (IA/HM) child is well behaved both at home and at school. For most of the children I've worked with, these gains are sufficient to help them get along better with immediate family, teachers, and other children. Teachers and other children generally no longer dread it when your child walks into the room. Instead of being ostracized, criticized, and picked on, he is greeted with warm hellos and friendly smiles. This doesn't necessarily hold true for all children, however. Some children need additional help in learning how to get along better. In this chapter, we'll review some suggestions you can work on with your child to help him develop better social skills.

THE SOCIAL LIFE OF THE ADD/ADHD (IA/HM) CHILD

Generally ADD/ADHD (IA/HM) children aren't liked by teachers and other children. They are considered to be obnoxious, and as a result they are treated badly. Other children tease and taunt them. Things are said that are intended to get a reaction out of the ADD/ADHD (IA/HM) child. The stronger the reaction, the more ammunition the other children have for even stronger taunts. This negative cycle may continue until the ADD/ADHD (IA/HM) child becomes aggressive. Out of frustration and loss of all emotional control, he may lash out furiously. Sadly, this only confirms for the other children what a misfit the ADD/ADHD (IA/HM) child really is. He also frequently faces not being chosen for team sports, or being chosen last. It is humiliating, crushing, and scarring to be treated this way.

Teasing and taunting have escalated to an out-of-control epidemic in our schools. Children who engage in this behavior seem to be experts at finding weaknesses in other children. They have honed their attacks to a razor-sharp cutting edge. It seems to be a consistent pattern that children who commit school shootings have histories of being neglected and of being targets for severe teasing and taunting. I'm not excusing what they do. I am pointing out that teachers, principals, headmasters, and parents need to actively address this problem. We must begin training children to not engage in teasing and taunting and to develop a heightened sensitivity to the feelings of others. It is a practice that must be stopped.

School bullies love to target their ADD/ADHD (IA/HM) classmates because they know that no one likes these children, and the bully can jockey himself into a position of importance by goading them. Sometimes the bully may go even farther, making the ADD/ADHD (IA/HM) child give him something as payment not to get beaten up. It's an act of submission designed to humiliate. The bully may go even farther by making the ADD/ADHD (IA/HM) child do something degrading, like kneeling in homage or contrition. I had one little boy who was forced to lick the shoe of the bully. Why isn't being a bully classified as a disease? Can a child ever heal from such terrible treatment?

The ADD/ADHD (IA/HM) child is constantly subjected to subtle reminders of her unacceptability. The teacher may not smile when she walks in. She avoids calling on her for answers. Her tone of voice may become sarcastic or may convey utter disgust. Subtle acts of rejection can be powerfully painful. Teachers generally don't mean to behave this way. They may even be unaware of their automatic reactions. It's difficult to be nice to a child who behaves obnoxiously, disrupts the class, and makes the teacher's workday miserable.

You as a parent may inadvertently be doing the same thing as the teachers. Don't feel guilty; it's really hard not to react. I know you love your child, but I bet there are times you resent him. Hopefully, now that you've seen considerable progress, your feelings are much more positive. You feel better, your child responds more positively, and he probably feels better too.

There are several ways you can teach your child to get along even better. Not all children need this extra instruction, but some children do need a little extra help.

WHAT TO DO TO HELP YOUR CHILD LEARN NEW BEHAVIORS

Whatever you do, don't try to teach your child all these social skills in one sitting—that's overwhelming. Work on one skill at a time. Teach her through quiet discussion, and perhaps make a game by role-playing.

In role-playing, have your child be the teacher, or any person she's been having trouble with, and you play your child. Show her the type of behavior that causes her problems. This is called *mirroring*. Have her react as the other person would. Then reverse roles and model how to handle it better.

Let your child be herself, and you be the teacher. Talk about how you feel when she behaves poorly. Ask her to try the new ways of behaving that we're going to discuss. Let her practice these new behaviors with you as preparation for actually attempting them in the "real world."

LESSON 1 — USE SILENCE

Other children like a quiet child more than a loud one. Instead of yelling, "Pick me!" teach your child to remain silent. It's hard to do, but over time it helps a child be more readily accepted. Other children will seek out the quiet child and rebuff the noisy ones.

LESSON 2 — DON'T TRY SO HARD TO HAVE YOUR WAY

Don't be bossy. Often, the ADD/ADHD (IA/HM) child will try to dominate or dictate the activities of a group. Teach your child to make suggestions in a normal tone and then let the others decide. He then follows the suggestion with silence. Teach him that being pushy and bossy is a turnoff to other children. Practice various situations with your child.

LESSON 3 — BE PATIENT

It takes time for other children to warm up to someone they have previously rejected. Let the silence and not being pushy work for your child. If he is meeting a new group, it takes a few weeks of "feeling out" the new kid before the group gradually accepts him. If your child's current group has persecuted him, then it will take a while to reverse the process. If your child learns to use silence, patience, and no longer being pushy to work for him, others will slowly begin to change their attitudes. Your child has to make a commitment to being very patient. It takes weeks for other kids to change their attitudes. Talk with your child daily about their progress and encourage him to remain patient. I've seen this reversal work for ADD/ADHD (IA/HM) children many times. Silence and not being pushy removes your child from being a favored target. In the normal course of daily activities, the other children will gradually let him play with them. They will slowly forget the old obnoxious kid and rediscover the new nice kid. Surprisingly, other children will detect that your child is really trying to be nice, and often they will accept and respect his efforts. It works, but your child will need lots of encouragement to be patient and let the process gradually unfold.

Lesson 4—Don't try to be a know-it-all in class

The ADD/ADHD (IA/HM) child often calls out answers in class and, because of his hastiness, he may misunderstand the teacher's question and answer incorrectly. He may raise his hand, calling out, "Me, me, me" or "Teacher, Teacher, Teacher." This is a turnoff to both the teacher and other children. Teach your child to moderate answering questions and to learn the art of active listening. Have him take his time to carefully understand the question asked by the teacher and make certain he knows the correct answer before raising his hand.

I've deliberately instructed ADD/ADHD (IA/HM) children *not* to answer questions, even if they know the answer. At first, this may sound rather odd. But the goal is to improve relationships. By pacing answering questions and raising his hand, your child can stop drawing unpopular attention to himself and becoming a target. Pacing and being more calm and "laid back" in answering questions in class helps improve relationships. Again, this involves a little more silence and a little less trying so hard. This is called "trying too hard." That's exactly what the ADD/ADHD (IA/HM) child does—he tries too hard. Impress on your child that "trying too hard" is what makes other children not like him. He tries so hard to be liked, respected, and popular that he causes a backlash: He is considered obnoxious and unlikable. More silence, less pushiness, and more patience in the classroom will help considerably in changing attitudes toward your child.

LESSON 5 — DON'T LOSE YOUR TEMPER

This is a crucial message to teach your child. A good rule is *one loss of temper equals one month of being picked on*. The underlying emotion when your child loses her temper is usually fear. Teasing and taunting by other children results in a surge of adrenaline. Being afraid that the other children hate her and will reject her causes a fear response that in psychology we call a *fight or flight reaction*. When this happens and the rush of adrenaline occurs, your child starts to lose emotional control. Flight often is interpreted as being a coward, and your child usually rejects this as an option. Fight is then incorrectly interpreted as saving face. Within a short time, your child may begin screaming, threatening, and perhaps even hitting. This is exactly what the teasing and taunting were intended to do. Once your child loses control, he is a ready target for the group. The taunts get worse. Your child's temper gets worse. The humiliation gets worse. The scars get worse. Explain this whole process to your child, and that he can learn a new way to handle the taunting.

I find that it's useful to give ADD/ADHD (IA/HM)

children an analogy. I explain to them that when they are in a confrontation, they can think of handling the other kids as being like judo, where they use the other person's weakness to their advantage. Help your child understand that when a group is taunting him, the leader is trying to establish his importance or superiority to the group. That's usable information. A useful comeback is for your child to step up to the leader of the group and ask, "Does it make you feel like a big shot to hurt someone else? If it makes you feel so important, then just keep making fun of me!" Usually these two sentences are sufficient to take the wind out of the ringleader, and that's the end of the situation. This is a difficult thing for a child to do. Rehearsing it at home helps prepare him should the situation arise.

Tell your child that one loss of temper equals one month of taunting, and it will serve as a mental message he can keep in the forefront of his thoughts when facing a confrontation. It can help restrain his reactions. In addition, thinking about that two-sentence rebuttal serves as a useful tool for handling this stressful situation.

LESSON 6—LEARN TO BE WARM

It may surprise you that ADD/ADHD (IA/HM) children are often quite shy. Their boisterous behavior serves as a smoke screen to hide their fears of rejection. On the surface, they seem gregarious and controlling, but underneath they are terrified of rejection. They've had numerous occasions of actually being rejected, and each incident hurts and scars. A long history of such treatment leads to shyness.

Once we understand that they are shy, we can help them compensate in more constructive ways. Power, control, and dominance are not the way to win friends. Being warm and friendly works considerably better. A few simple suggestions can help your child make friends.

a. LOOK: Watch your child's ability to make eye contact. I'll bet you discover that she rarely looks directly at the person she's talking to. Have her practice looking you in the eye when talking to you. Teach her that good eye contact is important whenever she's talking to someone. It conveys a message that the other person is important and that she is interested in what the other person has to say.

b. ASK: The shy ADD/ADHD (IA/HM) child mistakenly believes that he must do all the talking. He works extra hard at trying to have a conversation with another child. This puts a lot of pressure on the ADD/ADHD (IA/HM) child to perform. Unfortunately, not only does his talkativeness not work well, it has the opposite effect of turning the other child off. Tell your child that other children don't always want to hear what he has to say; instead, they want to talk about themselves and what they consider important. This provides ammunition for another judo move. Teach him that the easiest way to make friends is to ask questions. Not too many, and not in a staccato, rapid fashion. A few introductory questions will help get the other child talking. He can ask a new child at school, "Where did you move from?" "Do you know anything about the school?" "What was your old school like?" "Have you met anyone yet?" "Do you like sports?" "What kind of things do you like to do?"

For reestablishing relations with children your child has had problems with, ask questions like, "Did you watch the Mets last night?" "What did you think of the math homework last night?" (Girl to girl): "I like that dress—can I ask where you got it?" When working with your child, get his ideas about questions he can ask other children. Practice with him. He may soon learn that once he gets the other child talking, the hardest part will be getting the other child to stop. Once he gets on a roll, the child will probably end up thinking your child is "pretty nice, once you get to know him."

A helpful thought for your child to keep in mind is, "They don't want to hear what you have to say. They want to do most of the talking. Let them." After a few successes your child's confidence will grow.

c. LISTEN: Getting the other child to talk is a helpful tool. Learning to listen actively can give your child another one. If she listens intently, then more and more questions about the other child's interests will arise. By asking questions in a truly sincere way, the other child will go on and on, and all the while she'll be thinking how great your child is.

Asking questions and listening carefully is a lot less stressful for your child than working excessively hard at performing for the other children, trying too hard to win them over. These techniques are easier and far more productive for your child in getting her affiliation needs met.

d. A GENTLE SMILE: Looking glad helps when your child sees a familiar face, but it is important to not overdo it. A gentle, soft smile conveys a warm and caring message.

ADD/ADHD (IA/HM) children overdo almost everything. Instead of showing a gentle, friendly demeanor, they often try to be the class clown, and typically they aren't very funny. They often come across as rude, crude, and obnoxious. Instead, advise them to be warm, quiet, and nice. Smile, but don't be a clown.

Some children do have an excellent sense of humor, and it's not my intention to crush such a marvelous ability. Observe your child, and see if her sense of humor is effective or self-defeating. If effective, then help her learn the appropriate times and places to act funny. The classroom is neither appropriate nor timely. Clowning in class is rude, disruptive, and very unlikable. Help your child rechannel her humorous skills to parties and get-togethers. But most ADD/ADHD (IA/HM) children aren't funny. Their attempts at humor only make them targets for the wrath of the other children. Help your child to be aware of this, to calm down, and to simply convey a warm smile.

LESSON 7 — DON'T TELL THE TEACHER

We often mistakenly advise children that whenever trouble arises, don't fight, just tell the teacher. Well, not fighting is of course important. But most situations do not merit telling the teacher. To do so will only earn the ADD/ADHD (IA/HM) child a reputation as a snitch and tattletale, and the other children will further rebuff him. He must learn to handle most difficult social interactions with his intelligence and skill. Some of the suggestions in this chapter will help, but they certainly don't cover all social situations. As each social difficulty arises, your child may be able to generate healthy solutions and act on them at the time of the problem. But if he can't, then work with him at home to practice thinking of solutions, and role-play. If you do this repeatedly, over time your child will build a repertoire of handy and healthy reactions to numerous difficult encounters. He'll learn to think on his feet. Continually running to the teacher or any other adult does not convey the message that you can handle most difficulties on your own.

There are two occasions where telling the teacher is the proper option: first, when your child is the victim of aggression; and second, when something dangerous is occurring—a child giving out pills, or a child carrying a gun. At such times, telling an adult is the exercise of good judgment. At others, your child will only improve social skills and confidence by handling difficult circumstances himself.

There is a great deal more we could cover about social-skills training. I've kept this chapter simple and short to make it easier for you to help your child. With control of his behaviors, with improvements in school performance and conduct, and with a few learnable social skills, your

ADD/ADHD (IA/HM) child should be doing better and better. Nevertheless, there is still more for us to cover. Your behaviors and your child's behaviors are governed by his and your beliefs. In the next chapter we're going to cover some of the most fundamental and crucial beliefs your child must have—these are called *values*.

CHAPTER 13

Value Education

W HY ARE WE EXPERIENCING an overwhelming escalation of the diagnosis of ADD/ADHD (IA/HM), about 500 percent since 1989? Why are so many children not paying attention in school? Why are more and more children increasingly misbehaving in school and at home? Why are children refusing to yield to authority figures and control their conduct when ordered to? As I stated earlier, in chapter 4, our stressful lifestyles make life very confusing for our children.

At the core of their confusion is the absence of a system of VALUES. Thomas Moore (1992) states that "the soul needs a particular world view and a particularly worked out scheme of values." Pope John Paul II, in his book *Crossing the Threshold of Hope*, states that "the young need guides. They want to be corrected and to be told yes and no." They need "a system of ethics."

Recall that in chapter 4 I discussed what is happening

all around our children. The extended family that helped teach strong fundamental values is too often lost. Our harried lifestyles don't allow time for parents to teach and instill a deep value system. Children are exposed to confusing value messages from the media. Association with misguided peers adds to their confusion over values. All these forces prevent children from learning a systematic, cohesive, and healthy set of values. We talked about several lifestyle changes that may help our families and our children. But stability and reduction of stress are only partial avenues for our most important goal: teaching our children solid, healthy, substantive, and meaningful *values*.

In this chapter, we'll discuss several core values that you might wish your child to learn. The child who deeply believes most, if not all, of these values will either discontinue being ADD/ADHD (IA/HM) or will never become ADD/ADHD (IA/HM) in the first place. Keep in mind that it is beliefs that govern one's behaviors.

VALUES TO TEACH

Before discussing specific values, it is essential to understand that we adults bear the burden of an important responsibility. We are role models to our children. We must live what we teach. Children are sensitive radar machines, and they can readily detect hypocrisy. Remember this: Don't do what you don't want your children to find out. In the 1960s, Al Bandura demonstrated repeatedly that modeling is perhaps the most powerful way children learn. What they observe in us, their role models, is what they learn. The purpose of the CSP conditioning is not merely to get ADD/ADHD (IA/HM) children's behaviors under control, but to control them so we can get the children's attention and teach them a system of values. I call the teaching of values *value education*.

Valuing Education

Earlier, we fully covered the importance of valuing education and instilling a love for reading. I only mention it here to keep in context all important values. Keep these two values in mind as core values that are equally as important as the others we'll be reviewing.

Love

To teach children to love, they must be loved. They need lots of time, attention, and nurturing. Love is the core theme of the *New Testament*. Matthew 22:34-40 teaches that loving God and loving one another are our two most important laws. If children learn to love deeply, then all else follows: They will treat their family with loving-kindness, they will treat other children with loving-kindness, and they will treat adults with loving-kindness. Conducting themselves that way eliminates the crude, disrespectful behaviors that are the hallmarks of ADD/ADHD (IA/HM).

This may sound odd coming from a psychologist, but I'm not alone. In their book *Teaching Your Children Values* Linda and Richard Eyre also emphasize love as a crucial value. James Dobson, in *Dare to Discipline*, states that children must learn to behave in loving ways. In his book *The*

Seven Habits of Highly Effective Families, Stephen Covey espouses the importance of helping children to feel and express love toward their family and others.

If you want your child to permanently change her behavior patterns, then keep this value in the forefront of her value education.

PEACE AND SERENITY

The ADD/ADHD (IA/HM) child is not at peace. He hasn't learned to value peace, quiet, and serenity. And this isn't a problem exclusive to ADD/ADHD (IA/HM) children—our children are bombarded with overstimulation. They sit in front of the television five to seven hours each day, they play video games, and they blast their CDs. I rarely see children taking a quiet walk or sitting quietly under a tree. Do you often hear, "I'm bored," about two minutes after his friends have left your house?

Teaching ADD/ADHD (IA/HM) children to relish peace and quiet is very important. If they are calm inside, they won't rush impatiently from one activity to another. They won't create chaos in their path.

The Eyres call this value "peaceability." They emphasize creating a peaceful environment in our homes by talking softly and listening to soft music. I add to this: read together, take quiet walks with your child, cuddle, and have quiet talks at bedtime. Calm your child's world, and you'll help calm your child.

Help your child treasure the values of peace and serenity. These words are used in the Bible hundreds of times, indicating there's an important message for us to pay attention to. Thomas Moore tells us to simplify our lives to help make things more peaceful. This isn't a new concept; philosophers have been teaching it for thousands of years. I still read Thoreau's *Walden* some evenings at bedtime to help calm me after a hectic day.

Notice that valuing peace could help your child considerably when practicing the social skills we discussed in the last chapter: silence, not trying too hard, not being pushy, not being impatient, not losing one's temper, not listening poorly.

SELF-DISCIPLINE

Albert Ellis, our modern equivalent of Sigmund Freud, has dramatically altered the direction of psychotherapy for the last thirty years. Psychologists used to believe that patients with emotional and behavioral problems only had to lie on a couch and talk about their problems to get better. Ellis has taught that this does not change anything. He has taught that it takes considerable self-discipline in controlling one's behaviors, thoughts, and beliefs to feel better. Therapy, he believes, is not magic, and merely talking to a therapist will not make one better. The patient has to exert deliberate and conscientious control over behaviors and thinking patterns if she ever wishes to feel better.

This same rule applies to ADD/ADHD (IA/HM) children. They suffer at the hands of others, and they fail in school, which is painful. To stop the hurting, we must help them adopt the value of self-discipline. Things will get better for them if they take responsibility and judiciously practice behaving better and working hard in school.

The CSP helps to get them under control, and the changes it produces bring reinforcements from teachers, peers, and parents. To sustain these wonderful gains, ADD/ADHD (IA/HM) children must also learn to assume responsibility for what will continue happening in their lives. Only self-control, self-discipline, hard work, and practice will facilitate the continuation of the better feelings they are now experiencing.

The CSP helps until about the age of eleven. After that, a child discovers his power to control his environment. If he uses his control for good purposes, he will benefit emotionally. If he blames everyone else for his problems and loses self-control, the suffering he experienced as an ADD/ADHD (IA/HM) child will return. Help him understand that it is his choice to be self-disciplined or to return to the failures and pain he so long suffered. The value of self-discipline is essential for continued successful living. Right now we control his world; later he does. Our work with him is not complete until he makes the transition to a firm belief in self-discipline.

Stephen Covey has created an interesting play on words. He states that being *responsible* means being *response able*, or, as he says, "Choose how [you want] to be." Laura Schlessinger (1998) places great importance on self-discipline and responsibility. She states that often emotional pain is deserved because people choose to behave irresponsibly. She claims that if one wants the hurt to stop, then one must start behaving responsibly. To me, childhood is the time to begin training in self-discipline and responsibility.

FUTURE GOALS

Much of my practice, teaching, writing, and research focuses on teenagers. All too often, I meet teens who have few interests, confused values, and no care or concern about what to do with their lives. If I give them a vocational test to help decide future goals, too many of them show no inclinations, interests, or values that match with any professions. The tests show that all they care about is being with their friends, smoking cigarettes, and "hanging out." They are without goals.

Parental influence and guidance in developing a goal-oriented perspective is an important ingredient in raising our children. If a child develops important goals about education, career aspirations, and family, then her behavior will be directed toward achieving those goals. But parents must actively help their children explore and develop what these goals will be. Unfortunately, too many parents are passive. They assume the school will take care of these matters. The reality is that that these values should be developed in the family.

I find that ADD/ADHD (IA/HM) children have poorly developed ideas about their future. They hate schoolwork, and they don't understand why they have to do it. If there is no direction, purpose, and meaning in life, there is no motivation to pay attention, work hard, and behave well. There must be reasons for them to do these things. In psychology this is called *attribution theory*, which means people must have good reasons before they are willing to engage in certain behaviors. If a child has developed strong goals, she will have underlying reasons to sustain her for the many years of hard work necessary for her schooling. Goal orientation provides motivation.

Do you want your child to be a farmer, a carpenter, an engineer, a professor, a mechanic, or whatever? Then work with him in cultivating these interests. If a father and son work side by side repairing a car, then the child's goals and interests are being cultivated. If a mother occasionally takes her daughter to her place of work, she is helping her daughter explore potential interests. My daughter used to assist her mother, who is a dentist, in the office. This helped my daughter decide that she did *not wish* to be a dentist. But, like her mother, she did decide to go as far with her education as she possibly could.

When my sons and I visited the American Museum of Natural History in New York last year, we discussed the professions that were necessary to compose the exhibits. I was helping them think about possible goals and directions for their lives. It takes this patient nurturing and deliberate effort to help them formulate *ballpark* ideas of what they want to do. Don't assume it will automatically happen. Help it happen.

Our earlier discussion about how to make education an important value incorporates many of the steps that can also help your child think about his future. Use them as guidelines for taking an active, enriching role with your child.

HARD WORK

I believe the value of hard work is fading in importance in American youth. The work ethic was a fundamental belief that helped create the greatness of this country. Sadly, less and less importance is placed on it. Each year an increasingly large number of my students work hard at not working hard. My fellow professors frequently complain about the same trend. More and more, I hear excuses for incomplete assignments; I see eyes downcast during discussion, and I know that students haven't prepared for class; I receive too many papers that reflect little effort in preparation. Most of my adolescent patients state plainly that they hate school and they hate work. All that seems important to them is to stay on the telephone and gossip. ADD/ADHD (IA/HM) children will spend hours feigning an inability to study or do their homework. They moan and groan in an effort to convince their parents that they can't do the work. Often they succeed in manipulating the parent to do the actual organizing, problem solving, deep concentration, and hard work to complete an assignment. If they're successful at getting the parent to do the work, and most of the time they are, then their only effort is to copy what the parent dictates. They've invested as little mental effort as possible, and they get away with it. Only the parent winds up learning the material.

To achieve future goals, two ingredients are essential—talent and hard work. Most ADD/ADHD (IA/HM) children have the talent, but they refuse to do the hard work. I teach children that hard work is an essential ingredient for personal happiness. This is a recurring theme in psychology, philosophy, and theology. When one focuses on one's work, then one cannot focus on things that are troubling. Albert Ellis emphasizes that "industrious occupation" is an essential ingredient for mental well-being. He states that it is one way to stay away from neurotic thoughts.

Future goals cannot be achieved without hard work. I

often discuss with my ADD/ADHD (IA/HM) patients who are older than eight the concept of "I could have been!" I share with them many stories of adults who came to see me, regretting what they failed to achieve in life. They had chosen a softer path rather than hard work; consequently, they spend the rest of their lives toiling at jobs they hate. They long for the career they wish they had pursued. They feel that they have talent that was never developed. I tell children one of the greatest secrets of a happy life is to spend one's workday doing what one loves and trying to be better at it than anyone else.

Many years ago I would spend an occasional day at Fairfield University watching the old New York Giants football team in training camp. I even had casual conversations with the players, and I learned a very important lesson. The great names in the sport at that time were Frank Gifford, Y. A. Tittle, and Hugh McElhenny, and they were not great by accident. If the team had to do fifty push-ups, they did two hundred. If the team ran one mile around the track, they ran five. When the team left the practice field, they stayed and continued to practice. They not only had the talent, but they also had the drive and willingness to work hard at being the best they could be. This is a magical secret that I wish more children would learn.

I often ask ADD/ADHD (IA/HM) children how they feel when a test is in front of them and they haven't studied. How do they feel having tests and homework repeatedly returned with failing grades? The only way to stop these painful feelings is to decide to do the work with all their heart and energy. Once they try this new approach, many of them tell me how great they feel when better grades actually begin to happen. They report that they feel so much better when they tackle their work with great vigor instead of avoiding it.

During a promotion ceremony at my sons' karate school, their instructor told them, "Pay attention to how great and proud you feel today. Remember the hard work you put in getting to this day. Learn that this is what it will take to have these feelings in all things that you do." Many of the children listened intently.

There are many other important values we could discuss, such as honesty and integrity, but the ones covered in this chapter were chosen as perhaps most relevant in helping a child curtail the ADD/ADHD (IA/HM) habits.

In the next and final chapter, we'll review the life changes suggested in this book that make the CSP successful. I wish to summarize for you the essential elements to focus on in order to maintain the successes you're now seeing in your former ADD/ADHD (IA/HM) child.

CHAPTER 14

Review of the Major Changes of the Caregivers' Skills Program

T HIS CHAPTER reviews the major features of the CSP, which produce substantial changes in ADD/ADHD (IA/HM) children without any resort to stimulants or amphetamine medications. Consider this a checklist to help you implement all the important parts of the program.

YOUR CSP CHECKLIST

Mark the boxes at the left of each item to be certain you're carrying out the essential elements of the CSP.

☐ 1. Treat your child as normal and not diseased. If you assume he or she is diseased, you'll do all the wrong things that other programs recommend. Remember, these programs don't get good results. In addition, your child will be convinced that he has a disease and will believe he has a handicap and will be a mental invalid for the rest of his life. This is rubbish. The ADD/ADHD (IA/HM) name is only a label that will disappear forever once you help him change.

☐ 2. Your child should not be taking any medications, including stimulants, tranquilizers, and antidepressants. Remember, these are risky for your child's health, and because they blunt your child's behaviors they will reduce the occurrences of behaviors that are essential for retraining your child. If the behaviors don't occur, we can't help him learn new habits.

☐ 3. Stop the excessive coaxing, reminding, cueing, helping, pleading, and warning. These practices focus on preceding events, as recommended by other popular approaches, and contribute to making your child helpless and dependent.

☐ 4. Control the consequences of your child's behaviors. Make him remember what will happen if he controls himself, that is, reinforcement, or if he fails to control himself, which will be discipline.

☐ 5. The CSP requires that you become superactive in the practice of reinforcing behaviors. Active praise is the key to success. This program requires that you "roll up your sleeves" and work hard if you want your child to change, be happy, and stay off the drugs.

☐ 6. Work on all Target Behaviors. Being thorough, comprehensive, and getting all Target Behaviors under control is a crucial part of the CSP.

☐ 7. Don't post rules. An important component of the CSP is to make your child think actively. All the reminding and coaxing in other programs keeps your child dependent and helpless. It's important to eliminate the Not Thinking cognitive component of ADD/ADHD (IA/HM).

☐ 8. Don't use a Token Economy program. It is an artificial and inappropriate way to raise a child. Posted rules and the physical presence of tokens contribute to cognitive dependency.

☐ 9. Do not use material reinforcers. These only serve to teach your child the false value of being paid for behaviors he should engage in, as a part of the normal course of family interactions. The only exceptions to this rule are for aggression and lying, which can be more difficult for ADD/ADHD (IA/HM) children to get under control.

☐ 10. Don't permit testing, preparatory, or anticipatory Target Behaviors. Do not allow a hint of a misbehavior. In other words, don't allow your child to test you. Such a stringent requirement forces your child to pay more careful attention to her behaviors and remember what to do at all times and in all settings. This requirement helps eliminate the Not Thinking habit of the ADD/ADHD (IA/HM) child.

☐ 11. Get *all* Target Behaviors under control at home *before* starting any school intervention. Establish yourself as the boss. Remember that in over 80 percent of the cases, school behavior automatically improves. This is a far greater percentage than with any other program, because the ADD/ADHD (IA/HM) child learns that you are the boss, you mean business, and she will face consequences enforced by you if she continues not to pay attention and to misbehave in school.

☐ 12. Do not permit your child to be placed in smaller "special needs" classes. He is normal, and he should be with normal kids. The increased individual attention in smaller classes only enhances the characteristic cognitive dependency of the ADD/ ADHD (IA/HM) child.

☐ 13. Do not sit with your child when she is doing homework. Supervision reinforces task, cognitive/ behavioral, and emotional dependency. She *can* do her homework, and with enforcement of contingencies she *will* do her homework. Only serve as a helpful resource for things that are apparently too difficult for your child to figure out on her own.

☐ 14. Do not coach or remind your child how to behave before going into a public place or any other setting. This only reinforces "not thinking" and cognitive/behavioral dependency.

CORRECT TIME OUT PROCEDURES

☐ 15. Do not give warnings or count "1-2-3 Time Out" before sending your child to Time Out. Doing so only contributes to cognitive/behavioral dependence. Your child will only learn compliance instead of learning active vigilance of his conduct. In addition, this prolonged interaction reinforces the Target Behavior.

☐ 16. Do not bargain or back down once the command "Go to Time Out" is given. If you do, you will teach your child to test you continually. She'll discover that she can test your limits and push you as far as she can.

☐ 17. Keep all interactions prior to Time Out to an absolute minimum. Any discussion or argument reinforces the Target Behavior occurring at that moment. "Go to Time Out" is all that should be necessary.

☐ 18. Require that she immediately comply with going to Time Out or she will receive a spanking. *You are the boss.*

☐ 19. After Time Out, insist that he tell you what he did wrong. This necessitates his active vigilance, awareness, and memory, a primary goal for working with the ADD/ADHD (IA/HM) child. If he can't remember, back he goes.

☐ 20. Send him back to Time Out if he misbehaves on the way. You are the boss, and the typical ADD/ADHD (IA/HM) testing behaviors should not be permitted.

☐ 21. Require your child to perform the correct behavior after she's told you what she did wrong. Again, establish yourself as the one in charge.

☐ 22. Use Time Out in all settings. Remember that when your ADD/ADHD (IA/HM) child learns to behave correctly everywhere, you can feel free to take him more places with you. You can enjoy each other's company more and have more fun together.

☐ 23. Teach your child to value education and to love reading. Learning these values is essential early in your child's life, or his lack of interest in school and his unwillingness to control his behaviors will return.

☐ 24. Teach your child a healthy and strong set of values.

☐ 25. Give your child lots and lots of love.

MY FINAL THOUGHT

Putting amphetamines into the bodies of our children is wrong. However, I can understand the frustration of parents, teachers, and doctors and the reasons for using them. This book and the Caregivers' Skills Program provide a true and effective alternative for the first time. I pray with all my heart that this book results in a dramatic decline in the prescribing of Ritalin and all other mind-controlling drugs for all children. I pray that other psychologists and psychiatrists will engage in more research on the techniques I present here, to make them even more effective and to reduce the reliance on drugs. I pray that physicians will prescribe this book instead of drugs as a first line of treatment. I pray that this book gives parents the alternative they've been seeking and that they may have a healthier and happier child. God bless our children.

REFERENCES

Amen, K. G., J. H. Paldi, and R. A. Thisted. 1993. Brain SPECT imaging. *Journal of the American Academy of Child and Adolescent Psychiatry* 32: 1080–81.

American Psychiatric Association (APA). 1968. *Diagnostic and statistical manual of mental disorders.* 2d ed. Washington, D.C.: APA.

———1980. *Diagnostic and statistical manual of mental disorders.* 3d ed. Washington, D.C.: APA.

———1994. *Diagnostic and statistical manual of mental disorders.* 4th ed. Washington, D.C.: APA.

Arnold, L. E., K. Kleykamp, N. Votolato, and R. A. Gibson. 1994. Potential link between dietary intake of fatty acids and behavior: Pilot exploration of serum lipids in attention deficit hyperactivity disorder. *Journal of Child and Adolescent Psychopharmacology* 4: 171–82.

Auci, D. L. 1997. Methylphenidate and the immune system. *Journal of the American Academy of Child and Adolescent Psychiatry.* 36: 1015–16.

Baldessarini, R. J. 1985. *Chemotherapy in psychiatry: Principles and practice.* Cambridge, Mass.: Harvard University Press.

Bandura, A. 1981. In search of pure unidirectional determinants. *Behavior Therapy* 12: 30–40.

———1986. *Social foundations of thought and action: A social cognitive theory*. Englewood Cliffs, N.J.: Prentice-Hall.

Barkley, R. A. 1981. *Hyperactive children: A handbook for diagnosis and treatment*. New York: Guilford Press.

———1990. *ADHD: A handbook for diagnosis and treatment*. New York: Guilford Press.

———1991. Attention deficit hyperactivity disorder. *Psychiatric Annals* 21: 725–33.

———1995. *Taking charge of ADHD: the complete authoritative guide for parents*. Boys Town, Neb.: Boys Town Press.

Barkley, R. A., and C. E. Cunningham. 1978. Do stimulant drugs improve the academic performance of hyperkinetic children? *Clinical Pediatrics* 17: 85–92.

Baughman, F. 2000. In a personal communication.

Berkow, R., ed. 1997. *The Merck manual of medical information*. Whitehouse Station, N.J.: Merck and Co.

Bradley, C. 1937. The behavior of children receiving Benzedrine. *American Journal of Psychiatry* 94: 577–85.

Brasfield, W. 1999. Workshop presented by the Virginia Psychological Association, October 1999.

Breggin, P. R. 1991. *Toxic psychiatry*. New York: Saint Martin's Press.

Breggin, Peter R. 1998. *Talking back to Ritalin: What doctors aren't telling you about stimulants for children*. Monroe, Maine: Common Coverage Press.

Brown, W. A., and B. W. Williams. 1976. Methylphenidate increases serum growth hormone concentrations. *Journal of Clinical Endocrinology* 43: 937–38.

Castellanos, F. X., J. N. Giedd, P. Eckburg, W. L. Marsh, et al. 1994. Quantitative morphology of the caudate nucleus in attention deficit hyperactivity disorder. *American Journal of Psychiatry* 151: 1791–96.

Comings, D. E., B. G. Comings, D. Muhleman, G. Dietz, B. Shahbahrami, D. Tast, E. Knell, B. Kocsis, R. Baumgarten, B. W. Kovacs, D. C. Levy, M. Smith, R. L.

Borison, D. D. Evans, D. N. Klein, J. MacMurray, J. M. Tosk, J. Sverd, R. Gysin, and S. D. Flanagon. 1991. The dopamine D2 receptor locus as a modifying gene in neuropsychiatric disorders. *Journal of the American Medical Association* 266: 1793–1800.

Cook, E. H. Jr., M. A. Stein, B. L. Leventhal. 1997. Family based association of attention-deficit/hyperactivity disorder and the dopamine transporter. In *Handbook of psychiatric genetics*, ed. K. Blum and F. P. Noble, 297-310. Boca Raton, Fla.: CRC Press.

Davison, G. C., and J. M. Neale. 1978. *Abnormal psychology: An experimental clinical approach*. New York: John Wiley & Sons.

———1994. *Abnormal psychology*. 6th ed. New York: John Wiley & Sons.

DeGrandpre, R. J. 1999. *Ritalin Nation: Rapid-Fire Culture and the Transformation of Human Consciousness*. New York: W. W. Norton.

Dulcan, M. 1994. Treatment of children and adolescents. In *The American Psychiatric Press textbook of psychiatry*. 2d ed., ed. R. Hales, S. Yudofsky, and J. Talbott, 1207-50. Washington, D.C.: APA.

Ebaugh, F. G. 1923. Neuropsychiatric sequelae of acute epidemic Encephalitis in children. *American Journal of Disease in Children* 25: 89–97.

Geringer-Woititz, J. 1983. *Adult children of alcoholics*. Deerfield Beach, Fla.: Health Communications.

Gibson, W. 1957. *The miracle worker: A play for television*. New York: Knots.

Giedd, J. N., F. X. Castellanos, B. J. Casey, P. Kozuch, et al. 1994. Quantitative morphology of the corpus callosum in attention deficit hyperactivity disorder. *American Journal of Psychiatry* 151: 665–69.

Greenblatt, J. M., L. C. Huffman, and A. L. Reiss. 1994. Folic acid in neurodevelopment and child psychiatry. *Progress* in *NeuroPsychopharmacology and Biological Psychiatry* 18: 647–60.

Greenspoon, J. 1955. The reinforcing effect of two spoken sounds on the frequency of two responses. *American Journal of Psychology* 68: 409-16.

Hallowell, E. M., and J. J. Ratey. 1994. *Driven to distraction: Recognizing and coping with attention deficit disorder from childhood through adulthood*. New York: Pantheon Books.

Heilman, K. M., K. K. Voeller, and S. E. Nadeau. 1991. A possible pathophysiologic substrate of attention deficit hyperactivity disorder. *Journal of Child Neurology* 6: S76–S81.

Hunter, D. 1995. *The Ritalin free child: Managing hyperactivity and attention deficits without drugs*. Fort Lauderdale, Fla.: Consumer Press.

Jacobovitz, D., L. A. Stroufe, M. Stewart, and N. Leffert. 1990. Treatment of attentional and hyperactivity problems in children with sympathomimetic drugs: A comprehensive review. *Journal of the American Academy of Child and Adolescent Psychiatry* 129: 677–88.

Joyce, P. R., R. A. Donald, M. Nicholls, J. H. Livesay, and R. M. Abbott. 1986. Endocrine and behavior responses to methylphenidate in normal subjects. *Life Successes* 34: 1701–11.

Kendall, P. C. 1996. *Cognitive therapy with children*. Workshop presentation presented in Richmond, Va.

Lahat, E., E. Avital, J. Barr, M. Berkovitch, et al. 1995. BAEP studies in children with attention deficit disorder. *Developmental Medicine and Child Neurology* 37: 119–23.

LaHaze, S. 1998. In a personal communication.

Levy, F. 1989. CNS stimulant controversies. *Australian and New Zealand Journal of Psychiatry* 23: 497–502.

Levy, F. 1991. The dopamine theory of attention deficit hyperactivity disorder. *Australian and New Zealand Journal of Psychiatry* 25: 277–83.

Lovaas, O. I. 1987. Behavioral treatment and normal educational/intellectual functioning in young autistic children. *Journal of Consulting and Clinical Psychology* 55: 3–9.

Mannuzza, S., R. G. Klein, A. Bessler, P. Malloy, and M. LaPadula. 1993. Adult outcome of hyperactive boys. *Archives of General Psychiatry* 50: 565–76.

Mates, J. A., and R. Gittelman. 1983. Growth of hyperactive children on maintenance regimen of methylphenidate. *Archives of General Psychology* 40: 317–21.

Maxmen, J. S., and N. G. Ward. 1993. *Psychotropic drugs fast facts.* 2d ed. New York: W. W. Norton.

Mayberg, H. 1998. *Today.* New York: National Broadcasting Corporation, 7 May.

Millerger, S., J. Biederman, S. V. Faralone, L. Chen, and J. Jones. 1997. ADHD is associated with early initiation of cigarette smoking in children and adolescents. *Journal of the American Academy of Child and Adolescent Psychiatry* 26: 37–44.

Mischel, W. 1968. *Personality and assessment.* New York: John Wiley & Sons.

Moore, Thomas. 1992. *Care of the soul.* New York: Harper-Collins.

Murphy, D. A., W. W. Pelham, and A. R. Lang. 1992. Aggression in boys with attention deficit hyperactivity disorder: Methylphenidate effects on naturally occurring aggression response to provocation, and social information processing. *Journal of Abnormal Child Psychology* 20: 451–65.

Nasrallah, H., et al. 1986. Cortical atrophy in young adults with a history of hyperactivity in childhood. *Psychiatry Research* 17: 241–46.

National Institutes of Health (NIH). 1998. ADHD consensus conference. Bethesda, Md.: NIH.

Odell, J. D., R. P. Warren, W. L. Warren, R. A. Burger, and A. Maciulis. 1997. Association of genes within the major histocompatibility complex with attention deficit hyperactivity disorder. *Neuropsychobiology* 35 (4): 181–86.

Parker, H. 1994. *The ADD hyperactivity workbook for parents, teachers, and kids*. Plantation, Fla.: Specialty Press.

Phelan, T. 1984a. *All about attention deficit disorder*. Glen Ellyn, Ill.: Child Management.

———1984b. *All about attention deficit disorder*. Glen Ellyn, Ill.: Child Management (Video).

———1984c. *1-2-3 magic! Training your preschoolers and preteens to do what you want*. Glen Ellyn, Ill.: Child Management.

———1984d. *1-2-3 magic! Training your preschoolers and preteens to do what you want*. Glen Ellyn, Ill.: Child Management (Video).

Physicians' Desk Reference. 1997. Oradell, N.J.: Medical Economics Co.

Pizzi, W. J., E. C. Rode, and J. E. Barnhart. 1986. Methylphenidate and growth: Demonstration of a growth impairment and a growth-rebound phenomenon. *Developmental Pharmacology and Therapeutics* 9: 361–68.

Rao, J. K., J. R. Julius, T. J. Blethen, and T. J. Breen. 1997. Idiopathic growth hormone deficiency and attention deficit disorder (ADD): Effect of methylphenidate and pemoline on GH therapy: The National Cooperative Growth Study Results.

Samango-Sprouse, C. 1999. Frontal lobe development in childhood. In *The human frontal lobes: Functions and disorders. The science and practice of neuropsychology series*, ed. B. L. Miller and J. L. Cummings, 584–603. New York: Guilford Press.

Schlessinger, L. 1998. The *Dr. Laura* radio show. Richmond, Va.: WRIC Broadcasting.

Sedvall, G. 1997. The current status of PET scanning with respect to schizophrenia. *Neuropsychopharmacology* 7 (1): 41–54.

Seligman, Linda. 1994. *DSM–IV: Diagnosis and treatment planning*. Virginia: American Counseling Association (Audio).

Shaywitz, B. A., S. E. Shaywitz, T. Byrne, D. J. Cohen, and S. Rothnian. 1983. Attention deficit disorder: Quantitative analysis of CT. *Neurology* 33: 1500–03.

Skinner, B. F. 1971. *Beyond freedom and dignity*. New York: Bantam.

Stein, D. B. 1998. A media presentation made at the convention of the American Psychological Association in San Francisco, Calif.

——1999. *Ritalin is not the answer: A drug-free, practical program for children diagnosed with ADD or ADHD*. San Francisco, Calif.: Jossey-Bass Publishers.

Stein, D. B., and S. Baldwin. 2000. Toward an operational definition of disease, in psychology and psychiatry: Implications for diagnosis and treatment. *International Journal of Risk and Safety in Medicine*, August.

Steiner, C. M. 1974. *Scripts people live*. New York: Grove Press.

Still, G. F. 1902. The Coulstonian lectures on some abnormal physical conditions in children. *Lancet* 1: 1008–82.

Strauss, A., and L. W. Lehtiner. 1947. *Psychopathology and education of the brain impaired child*. New York: Greene & Stratton.

Swanson, J. M., K. McBurnett, T. Wigal, L. J. Pfiffner, et al. 1993. Effect of stimulant medication on children with ADD: A review of reviews. *Exceptional Children* 60: 154–61.

Swanson, J. 1998. *The biological basis of ADHD*. Paper presented at the National Institutes of Health ADHD consensus conference, Bethesda, Md.

Thoreau, H. D. 1854. *Walden: Life in the Woods*. Boston: Tichnor & Fields.

Valenstein, E. 1998. *Blaming the brain: The truth about drugs and mental health*. New York: Free Press.

Webster-Stratton, C. 1990. Enhancing the effectiveness of self-administered videotape parent training for families with conduct-problem children. *Journal of Abnormal Child Psychology* 18: 479–92.

Weiner, I. B. 1982. *Child and adolescent psychopathology*. New York: John Wiley & Sons.

Witters, W., P. Venturelli, and G. Hanson. 1992. *Drugs and society*. 3d ed. Boston: Jones & Bartlett.

Wright, J. W. 1997. *Do we really need Ritalin?: A family guide to attention deficit hyperactivity disorder (ADHD)*. New York: Avon Books.

Yudofsky, S. C., R. E. Hales, and T. Ferguson. 1991. *What you need to know about psychiatric drugs*. New York: Ballantine.

Zametkin, A. J., T. Nordahl, M. Gross, A. C. King, W. C. Semple, J. Rumsey, S. Hamburger, and R. M. Cohen. 1993a. Cerebral glucose metabolism in adults with hyperactivity of childhood onset. *New England Journal of Medicine* 323: 1361–66.

Zametkin, A. J., L. L. Liebenauer, G. A. Fitzgerald and A. C. King. 1993b. Brain metabolism in teenagers with attention deficit hyperactivity disorder. *Archives of General Psychiatry* 50: 330–40.

Zimbardo, P. G. 1977. *Shyness, what it is, what to do about it*. Reading, Maine: Addison-Wesley.

Zimbardo, P. G., and S. Radl. 1981. *The shy child*. New York: McGraw-Hill.

Dr. David B. Stein is a professor of psychology at Long-wood College, a state college in central Virginia. He has an extensive list of research publications and professional presentations. His books include *Ritalin Is Not the Answer: A Drug-Free, Practical Program for Children Diagnosed with ADD or ADHD* and *Controlling the Difficult Adolescent: The REST Program (Real Economy Program for Teens)*. His workbook for helping parents with ADD/ ADHD children will soon be in bookstores.

Affectionately called Dr. Dave, he has won numerous honors and awards for his twenty-five years of devoted work in offering drug-free treatment and parenting alternatives for the most difficult and out-of-control children and teens. He has been listed in *Who's Who Among America's Teachers* for many years; he is a diplomate, the highest clinical rank in medicine and psychology; he was awarded the 2000 Outstanding Teacher and Scholar Award at Longwood; and his research on ADD/ADHD treatment was selected as one of the top ten for media coverage at the 1997 American Psychological Association convention. His book *Ritalin Is Not the Answer* was endorsed as required reading by all parents, educators, and doctors at the 2001 Ritalin Litigation Conference in New York. Since his work was featured in the recent text *Advances in Medicine*, pediatricians and family physicians are increasingly prescribing his books as an alternative to drugs, and they are reporting excellent results. His most important role, he says, is "being dad to three wonderful children."

Dr. Stein recently became a member of national columnist and writer John Rosemond's Affirmative Parenting team. He now answers reader's questions at the Affirmative Parenting Web site, www.rosemond.com, and he will be a featured writer for John's new magazine *Traditional Parent*. He is a highly sought after public speaker. Information about him, his speaking schedule, and how to arrange speaking engagements may be made by contacting Willie Rosemond at 704-864-1012 (ext. 12), or through whrosemond@aol.com.